SOCIAL
PERSPECTIVES

Junko Murao   Akiko Miyama

SANSHUSHA

音声ダウンロード＆ストリーミングサービス（無料）のご案内

https://www.sanshusha.co.jp/text/onsei/isbn/9784384335279/

本書の音声データは、上記アドレスよりダウンロードおよびストリーミング再生ができます。ぜひご利用ください。

1 ➡ 別売（採用時提供）の「教室用 CD」のトラック番号です。

001 ➡ Warm-up 1, 2 を収録した「音声ダウンロード＆ストリーミングサービス」の MP3 ファイル番号です。

はじめに

　新型コロナウイルス・パンデミックを経て、世界は大きく変わり、さまざまな分野においてより効率的で効果の出るやり方の模索が始まりました。私たちの情報の受信・発信の仕方も多様化している中、ChatGPT の登場により、瞬時に質問の解答を受け取れるサービスがある一方で、その情報の信憑性も問われる時代になりました。そのような時代に必要とされる能力とは、情報を選別し、素早く読み取る力と、本質を見抜く力ではないでしょうか。

　本書では、英字新聞やインターネットから興味深い英文素材を取り上げていますが、生きた英語に触れると共に、膨大な情報の中から必要な情報の要点を即座に把握できる速読・速聴能力を養えるような設問内容となっています。また、何度もメディアで取り上げられているような興味深い話題を選択していますので、関連情報を手に入れようという姿勢も養えます。

本書の使い方

　さて、当テキストの具体的構成ですが、**Warm-up**、**Reading**、**Comprehension**、**Summary** と巻末の **Vocabulary Quiz** の 5 セクションからなっています。以下に具体的に各セクションのねらいや学習法を説明していますので、本書使用の際に参考にしてください。

　まず、**Warm-up** では、TOEIC® テストなどの英語資格試験のための基礎力を養うべく、速聴・速読用の設問形式にしています。

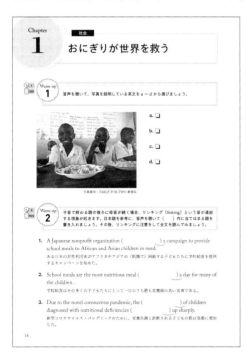

Warm-up 1

　TOEIC® テストの Part 1 の形式で、写真やイラストやグラフなどの視覚情報を利用して、章で扱っている**トピックのイメージを把握**します。後のセクションの背景知識を構築する大切なセクションです。

Warm-up 2

　語や句レベルのリスニング力を養うセクションです。発音規則をリスニング形式の問題を通して学習します。このセクションで扱う語句は、**後続セクションの重要表現**にもなっており、解答するだけでなく、しっかり覚えるようにしましょう。

Warm-up 3

　背景知識を構築するための**リスニング**の練習問題（問A）と、短い記事を用いた**拾い読み**の練習問題（問B）です。できるだけ辞書を引かずに、**速読・速聴**するように心がけてください。細部が聴き取れなくても、読み取れなくても、それが気にならない姿勢を養いましょう。そうすることで、長い英文を読んだり、聴いたりする場合の抵抗感がなくなります。

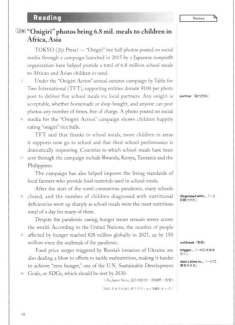

Reading

　いろいろな分野のトピックが選択されていますので、興味深く英語学習を続けることができるはずです。このセクションも、できる限り辞書に頼らず、**Warm-up** のセクションで培った背景知識をもとに推理力を働かせて読む癖をつけ、実社会で役立つ、**要点を把握しながら速読する**力を養うように心がけてください。難解な表現には注（ Notes ）を付けていますが、わからない表現が出てきたら、すぐ注を参照するのではなく、**あらかじめ意味を類推してから注で確認**するという読み方をしてください。

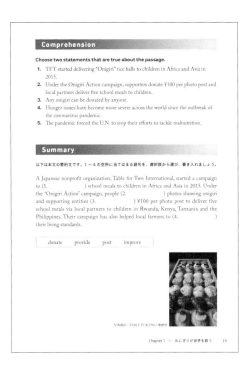

Comprehension

Reading セクションの**内容理解を確認**するセクションです。長文が苦手な人は、先にこのセクションに目を通し、**Reading** の内容を予測するのもよいでしょう。**Reading** のセクションは、逐語訳しないで、当セクションの答えを探すという**拾い読み**をすることで、**速読力を養う**ことができます。

Summary

Reading セクションの英文の要約文です。空所を埋めながら読み、本文の内容を理解できているかどうか確認することができます。

Vocabulary Quiz

巻末の **Vocabulary Quiz** は、**Reading** セクションで学んだ単語、熟語を復習し、定着させるためのクイズです。各章の総復習として利用し、着実に知識を積み上げていきましょう。切り取り式なので、提出用の課題としてもお使いいただけます。

当テキスト全章を学んだ後では、どんなニュースを眼にしても、テキストで学習をした手法を用いて、無意識的にウォームアップがなされ、重要情報を素早く読み取る力が養われていることでしょう。

著者

CONTENTS

英字新聞の読み方

　英字新聞記事は、「ヘッドライン（見出し）」「リード（書き出し）」「ボディー（本文）」のパートからなり、読者が短時間で必要な情報を手に入れることができるように、さまざまな工夫がなされています。どんな工夫があるか、各パート別に見てみましょう。

A　ヘッドライン

　ヘッドラインは、ニュースを最も簡潔に伝えるという役割を担っています。そのため思い切った省略や工夫が慣例的になされており、それを心得ていることが肝要です。また、ヘッドラインは読者を引きつける広告のような役割も果たしていますので、短いだけでなく、読者が魅力を感じるような表現の工夫もなされています。次に、慣例の特徴をまとめ、それらの特徴を含んだヘッドラインを例示します。

1　時制の用法

a. 過去・現在完了は現在形で表す。

Study connects climate hazards to 58% of infectious diseases

　ある研究によると、ヒト感染症のうち、58% にあたる症例が、気候変動に関連する異常気象によって悪化しているようだというニュースのヘッドラインです。「関連付けた」という過去の出来事を伝える動詞を connects と現在形で表しています。ニュースが「過去のもの」という印象になったり、数字も古いと読者に感じさせたりしないための工夫です。このように、多くのヘッドラインでは、ニュースの新しさや、臨場感を強調するために、しばしば動詞の過去形の代わりに現在形が用いられます。

b. 未来は主に「to + 動詞」で表す。

9-yr-old in Osaka to become youngest pro Go player in history

　大阪市の小学 3 年生が、史上最年少でプロ囲碁棋士として採用されることを伝えたニュースです。未来の出来事に will を使用するより、不定詞を用いた方が切れ味の良い表現となります。will をあえて用いる場合は、意志未来になることが多いです。

2 分詞の用法

a. 現在分詞は主に近い未来・予定を表す。

Hair donations booming in Japan but know-how still lacking

　現在分詞（booming, still）の前で be 動詞 are、is が省略されています。省略することで、語数が少なくなります。それで活字を大きくすることができ、よりヘッドラインが強調されます。「be 動詞＋現在分詞」は、進行状態を表したり、近接未来となったりします。ここでは、日本では、がんなどで苦しむ子どもたちのために、髪の毛を提供して医療用ウィッグを作る取り組みが近い将来「増えることが期待されています（booming）」が、提供者の知識不足や製造業者が現在「不足している（lacking）」という話題を取り上げたニュース記事のヘッドラインです。

b. 過去分詞は主に受動態を表す。

Gloves created to increase hand strength without any training

　be 動詞 are が、過去分詞（created）の前で省略されています。パーキンソン病患者やアスリート向けに指の筋肉を鍛えるための手袋が開発されたという最新科学技術を伝えたニュースです。特別な訓練は必要なく、日々の動きで筋肉が鍛えられるのはありがたいですね。

3 語数を少なくするためのさまざまな工夫

a. 冠詞・be 動詞・代名詞の所有格は省略する。

Bookstore with no actual store celebrates decade of selling books

　この例では、bookstore と decade の前に冠詞の a が省略されています。ある書店が実際の店舗ではなく、オンライン店舗で書籍を売り、10 周年を祝うことができたことを伝えています。「いか文庫」と呼ばれるこのエア文庫は書店の生き残りにある可能性を示すことができると期待されています。

b. コンマにより and を省略する。

Official: China mining more coal but increasing wind, solar

　当局発表によると、中国は石炭採掘量を増やすが、風力・太陽光発電も増やすというニュース報道ですが、wind と solar の間に and が省略され、代わりにコンマが用いられています。and を使用するより、切れ味の良い語調となります。

c. コロンを使用して発言者（情報源）と発言（情報）内容を分けて示すことがある。**Say** などの伝達動詞を省略する手法。

Study: Japanese pheromone could be used to repel invasive fire ants

　日本の在来種のフェロモンが外来種のヒアリ撃退に使えるかもしれないということが、ある研究で述べられていることを伝えるニュースのヘッドラインです。says の代わりにコロン (:) が使用されています。

4 好まれる短い語

a. ピリオドによる短縮

Tokushima Pref. strives to turn 'forest caviar' into juicy new local specialty

　徳島県が「森のキャビア（finger lime のこと）」をジューシーな新名物に育てることに取り組んでいるというニュースですが、Pref. は Prefecture の省略です。

b. 短縮語の使用

Repair workers turn up 400-yr-old chisel found left under roof of Kyoto temple

　national や international などの頻出語は、natl や intl のように短縮されることがあります。このヘッドラインでは、京都の寺の補修工事のとき、屋根裏で 400 年前のノミが発見されたということを伝えていますが、yr は year を短縮したものです。

c. 略語の使用

Tokyo Tech, TMDU to merge in FY24

　東京工業大学（Tokyo Institute of Technology）と東京医科歯科大学（Tokyo Medical and Dental University）が 2024 年度（fiscal year）に統合することに合意したという内容のヘッドラインです。両大学名と年度という語句に略語が使用されています。

d. 短い綴り語の使用

Japan eyes rollout of free BA.5-tailored COVID-19 shots next week

　日本政府は、来週から BA.5 に合わせた COVID-19 の無料接種を始めることを計画していることを伝えるニュース。「計画する」という意味の単語には、plan to や attempt to などがありますが、eye のように短い綴り語を使用することで、ヘッドラインの文字数削

減に役立ちます。ヘッドラインは短くすればするほど、文字も大きくすることができメッセージを伝える威力も増します。

ヘッドラインによく用いられる短い綴り語

accord	協定	laud	賞賛する	quest	追求する
body	団体	loom	迫る	rap	非難する
boost	上げる	map	計画する	row	論争
coup	クーデター	mark	示す	rush	急ぐ
curb	抑制（する）	mart	市場	score	非難する
cut	削減（する）	nip	阻止する	slash	削除する
eye	注目する／もくろむ	nix	否認する	slay	殺す
head	率いる	nuke	核兵器	stem	阻止する
hike	引き上げる	OK	承認する	talk	会談（する）
ink	締結する	oust	追放する	term	称する
key	重要な	pact	協定	top	越す
lash	攻撃する	poll	世論調査	vie	争う

5 読者を引きつける表現の工夫

The war drags on as Putin pushes his people 'into the river'

　読者が知っている映画や本、あるいは有名人のセリフ、名言などをもじってヘッドラインが書かれることがあります。特に、意見記事やコラムのヘッドラインにこの手法がよく用いられます。これは、朝日新聞の『天声人語』の 2022 年 9 月 30 日のコラム「反戦歌を」の英語版（『天声人語』の英語版は The Asahi Shimbun の Vox Populi で読むことができる）に付けられていたヘッドラインです。『天声人語』の題名は「反戦歌を」となっていますが、英語版の題名には変更が加えられています。『天声人語』の筆者は、コラム中で、ロシアによるウクライナ侵攻のニュースに日々接するうちに反戦歌を口ずさむことが増えたと述べています。そして、米国のフォーク歌手ピート・シーガーが歌ったベトナム戦争下の反戦歌「腰まで泥まみれ（Waist Deep in the Big Muddy）」を取り上げ、ウクライナ戦争に類似した状況があるのではと語っています。Waist Deep in the Big Muddy では、戦闘に向かうある部隊が、川を歩いて渡ろうとするのですが、川が予想以上に深いために腰まで泥水につかってしまうという状況が描かれています。この時点で、軍曹は、部隊長に引き返すべきかどうか尋ねます。隊長は、過去の経験で Big Muddy に首までつかるまで前進を続けても大丈夫だと答え、部隊にそのまま進むように命令します。

　英語版のヘッドライン中の into the river は、シーガーの歌の題名にある in the Big

Muddy を下敷きにした表現です。英語版の筆者は into the river に引用符をつけて、何かをもじっていますよという信号を読者に向けて発信しています。一方、読者はその信号を受け取り、コラムを読んで、なぜ引用符がついていたのか、腑に落ちるということになります。コラム中では、元歌の結末までは述べられていないのですが、実は、歌詞中では、軍曹の英断で、隊長以外の部隊全員が生還するという結末が述べられています。

B リード

　ニュース記事の書き出しの一段落目（リード）は記事の簡潔な要約で、5Ws（Who, What, When, Where, Why）と 1H（How）などの情報ができるだけ入るように書かれています。読者は、リードの部分の情報を読み、さらに先に記事を読み進めるかどうかを判断します。

1 ニュース記事のリード

　以下の記事には、どのような情報が入っているかを確認しましょう。

Crowdfunding drive seeks real armor for 'samurai corps' promoting west Japan castle

YONAGO, Tottori — A crowdfunding drive to acquire new armor for a "samurai corps" promoting the national historic site of the Yonago Castle ruins here is set to be launched on Oct. 19, with the aim of raising 1.5 million yen (about $10,000) in donations.

(The Mainichi)

---

who 　… 述べられていない
what 　… 国史跡・米子城跡で PR 活動をしている武者隊の甲冑衣装を新調するためのクラウドファンディングが始まった
when 　… 10 月 19 日に
where 　… 鳥取県米子市で
why 　… 150 万円の資金を集めるために
how 　… （ふるさと納税型の）寄付で

　通信社が配信する記事の場合、リードの冒頭に通信社名が付記されることがあります。BERLIN（AP）であれば、ベルリンより配信された AP 通信社の記事となります。主な通信社には以下のようなものがあります。上記記事は、通信社名が付記されていないので、

毎日新聞社の記事だということがわかります。

Associated Press Service	:AP 通信社　アメリカ
United Press International	:UPI 通信社　アメリカ
Interfax	:インテルファクス通信社　ロシア
Reuters	:ロイター通信社　イギリス
Jiji Press	:時事通信社　日本
Kyodo News	:共同通信社　日本
Xinhua News Agency	:新華社　中国
Agence France-Presse	:AFP 通信社　フランス

2 社説・論説記事 (editorial) のリード

　社説・論説記事は、一連のニュースの解説やそのニュースに対する意見を発表しています。従ってリードの部分では、当該ニュースの概要や背景がまとめられたり、ニュースに対する問題提起が行われたりします。ニュース記事と異なり、ある程度時間が経過してから書かれますので、読者がニュースについて情報を持っていることを想定し、ニュース記事のような細かい具体情報は省かれることが多いです。以下の社説のリードを見てみましょう。

Continued support vital to reshape basic research in Japan

The three natural science Nobels have been announced, but no Japanese scientists picked up prizes to follow last year's win. In recent years, there have been concerns about a decline in Japan's research capabilities. Continued support for basic science is necessary. *(The Japan News)*

　直前の自然科学のノーベル賞 3 賞発表のニュース報道を受けての社説のリードです。昨年に続き日本人科学者の受賞はなく、近年、日本の研究力の低下が懸念されていて、基礎科学への継続的な支援が必要であるという導入となっています。

　ニュース記事のリードのように、誰が、どのような賞を受賞したのかなどの詳細な情報は掲載されず、簡単にトピックの背景を紹介しているだけにとどめてあります。

C ｜ ボディー

　ニュース記事と社説・論説のボディーの構造は異なります。ニュース記事は、リードで

5Ws1H という最重要情報が示され、その後は、より些末な具体的情報を付加していくという構造を取ります。

　一方、社説・論説は、リードにおいて、取り上げられるニュースの概説や問題提起、次にそのニュースに対する意見や解説、最後に提起された問題に対する解決の提案などや結論が述べられるという構造となります。さらに、結論部では、しばしばニュースを一般化した視点でまとめられることもあります。ニュース記事のように最初に力点を置いて読むのではなく、記事全体を注意深く読む必要があります。上で取り上げた社説の結論部では、以下のように、「この（大学基金を立ち上げるという）構想の影響は、すでに現れていて、東京工業大学と東京医科歯科大学は、この基金の申請に向けて統合の協議を始めている。今後、政府や大学のトップが、この基金の効果的な使い方を検討し、研究能力の底上げに向けた戦略を練ることが期待される」と述べられていて、低下している日本の研究力底上げの一解決策を紹介し、未来への期待で締めくくられています。

The influence of the initiative can already be seen: Tokyo Institute of Technology and Tokyo Medical and Dental University have begun merger talks to apply for the fund. It is hoped that the government and university leadership will consider effective ways to use the fund and devise strategies to raise the level of research capabilities.

(The Japan News)

D　キャプション（説明文）

　記事の写真やイラストやグラフなどの視覚情報は、読者の興味を効果的に引きつける広告のような役割を果たしています。通常、これらの視覚情報には、キャプションと呼ばれる説明文が伴われます。

　以下の写真には ChatGPT を利用した実際のやり取りのパソコン画面が写っています。写真のキャプションでは、「質問やリクエストに対して、ChatGPT は人間のような返答をする」と説明されていますが、当該記事はメディアでしばしば取り上げられる ChatGPT が話題だということがわかります。

　一方、ヘッドラインには、「ある調査によると、日本の大学生の 32.4％が ChatGPT を利用していると回答した」と述べられています。この記事の場合、読者は写真とキャプション、さらにヘッドラインに目を通すことで、「教育現場での ChatGPT 利用に関する実態調査」についての内容だという予測ができ、記事を読む際の背景知識を効率的に構築することができます。

Survey: 32.4% of college students in Japan say they use ChatGPT

June 8, 2023 *(The Asahi Shimbun)*

ChatGPT gives human-like responses to questions and requests. (Masayuki Shiraishi)

社会

おにぎりが世界を救う

Warm-up
1

音声を聴いて、写真を説明している英文を a ～ d から選びましょう。

a. ☐

b. ☐

c. ☐

d. ☐

写真提供：TABLE FOR TWO 事務局

Warm-up
2

子音で終わる語の後ろに母音が続く場合、リンキング（linking）という音が連結する現象が起きます。日本語を参考に、音声を聴いて（　　）内に当てはまる語を書き入れましょう。その後、リンキングに注意をして全文を読んでみましょう。

1. A Japanese nonprofit organization (　　　　　　　　　) a campaign to provide school meals to African and Asian children in need.

   ある日本の非営利団体がアフリカやアジアの（飢餓で）困窮する子どもたちに学校給食を提供するキャンペーンを始めた。

2. School meals are the most nutritious meal (　　　　　　　) a day for many of the children.

   学校給食はその多くの子どもたちにとって一日のうち最も栄養価の高い食事である。

3. Due to the novel coronavirus pandemic, the (　　　　　　　) of children diagnosed with nutritional deficiencies (　　　　　　　) up sharply.

   新型コロナウイルス・パンデミックのために、栄養失調と診断される子どもの数は急激に増加した。

Warm-up 3A　音声（NPO 法人 TABLE FOR TWO International の行うキャンペーンの目標について）を聴いて、以下の文中の空所に適当な数字を書き入れましょう。

TABLE FOR TWO は、開発途上国の飢餓問題や先進国の肥満の問題の解決を目指している。彼らは、このプロジェクト始まって以来の最多となる、（1.　　　　）人の子どものための一年分の給食に当たる、（2.　　　　）食の給食を提供する目標を立てた。

Warm-up 3B　以下の英文（NPO 法人 TABLE FOR TWO International の活動について）を読み、質問に答えましょう。

　　Table for Two International (TFT) said more and more people in and outside Japan are taking part in the campaign as they can easily extend aid by simply posting photos on such social media as Twitter with the hashtag "#OnigiriAction" or on a dedicated website.

　　This year, the campaign is being held for a month through Nov. 6, bringing together a record 37 supporting entities, including major convenience store chain operator Seven-Eleven Japan Co. and the prefectural government of Miyagi, northeastern Japan.

(The Japan News, JIJI PRESS)

Notes　**extend aid**「援助する」　**dedicated**「専用の」　**entity**「団体」

Which of the following is true about the Onigiri Action campaign?

a. People can participate in the campaign by posting photographs.

b. This campaign lasts until the end of November.

c. A major convenience store chain is leading this campaign.

d. Many international companies will join this campaign.

⊚ 5 "Onigiri" photos bring 6.8 mil. meals to children in Africa, Asia

TOKYO (Jiji Press) — "Onigiri" rice ball photos posted on social media through a campaign launched in 2015 by a Japanese nonprofit organization have helped provide a total of 6.8 million school meals to African and Asian children in need.

5　Under the "Onigiri Action" annual autumn campaign by Table for Two International (TFT), supporting entities donate ¥100 per photo post to deliver five school meals via local partners. Any onigiri is acceptable, whether homemade or shop-bought, and anyone can post photos any number of times, free of charge. A photo posted on social

10　media for the "Onigiri Action" campaign shows children happily eating "onigiri" rice balls.

TFT said that thanks to school meals, more children in areas it supports now go to school and that their school performance is dramatically improving. Countries to which school meals have been

15　sent through the campaign include Rwanda, Kenya, Tanzania and the Philippines.

The campaign has also helped improve the living standards of local farmers who provide food materials used in school meals.

After the start of the novel coronavirus pandemic, many schools

20　closed, and the number of children diagnosed with nutritional deficiencies went up sharply as school meals were the most nutritious meal of a day for many of them.

Despite the pandemic easing, hunger issues remain severe across the world. According to the United Nations, the number of people

25　affected by hunger reached 828 million globally in 2021, up by 150 million since the outbreak of the pandemic.

Food price surges triggered by Russia's invasion of Ukraine are also dealing a blow to efforts to tackle malnutrition, making it harder to achieve "zero hunger," one of the U.N. Sustainable Development

30　Goals, or SDGs, which should be met by 2030.

(*The Japan News, JIJI PRESS* 一部抜粋・改変)

*2021 年までのおにぎりアクション実績にもとづく

partner「協力団体」

diagnosed with...「〜と診断された」

outbreak「勃発」

trigger...「〜の引き金を引く」

deal a blow to...「〜に打撃を与える」

Comprehension

Choose two statements that are true about the passage.

1. TFT started delivering "Onigiri" rice balls to children in Africa and Asia in 2015.
2. Under the Onigiri Action campaign, supporters donate ¥100 per photo post and local partners deliver five school meals to children.
3. Any onigiri can be donated by anyone.
4. Hunger issues have become more severe across the world since the outbreak of the coronavirus pandemic.
5. The pandemic forced the U.N. to stop their efforts to tackle malnutrition.

Summary

以下は本文の要約文です。1 ～ 4 の空所に当てはまる語句を、選択肢から選び、書き入れましょう。

A Japanese nonprofit organization, Table for Two International, started a campaign to (1.   ) school meals to children in Africa and Asia in 2015. Under the "Onigiri Action" campaign, people (2.   ) photos showing onigiri and supporting entities (3.   ) ¥100 per photo post to deliver five school meals via local partners to children in Rwanda, Kenya, Tanzania and the Philippines. Their campaign has also helped local farmers to (4.   ) their living standards.

donate	provide	post	improve

写真提供：TABLE FOR TWO 事務局

地下でコミュニケーション

Warm-up **1**

音声を聴いて、写真を説明している英文を a ～ d から選びましょう。

a. ❏

b. ❏

c. ❏

d. ❏

Warm-up **2**

等位接続詞 and/or は複数の語を列挙する場合によく使われますが、発音する際にはイントネーションに注意が必要です。いくつ列挙する場合でも、最後の語は上げ調子になります。日本語を参照し、（　　　）内に and か or を書き入れましょう。その後、下線部のイントネーションに注意をして全文を読んでみましょう。

1. The research group consists of researchers at Ehime University, Utsunomiya University, (　　　　　　　　　) the University of Leeds in Britain.

その研究グループは、愛媛大学と宇都宮大学、英国のリーズ大学の研究者で構成されている。

2. "Plant hormone" is a general term for compounds produced by plants that boost (　　　　　　　　) prevent growth, germination (　　　　　　　　) flowering.

「植物ホルモン」は、植物の成長や発芽、開花などを促進したり阻害したりする植物によって生み出される化合物の総称である。

3. Strigolactones are chemically unstable (　　　　　　　　) fragile.

ストリゴラクトンは化学的に不安定で、壊れやすい。

音声を聴いて、イネ科の植物がストリゴラクトンという植物のホルモンをどのように利用しているのかについて<u>述べられていないもの</u>はどれか、1 〜 4 から選びましょう。

1. 植物はストリゴラクトンを根の周辺で検知している。

2. ホルモンの分泌量を植物自体が決定している。

3. 植物はそのホルモンを使ってどこまでも根を伸ばせる。

4. ホルモンの加減によって植物自体が枝を出すかどうかを制御している。

 Notes determine...「〜を決定する」 branch「枝を出す」

以下の英文（ある研究グループの行っている植物に関する研究について）を読み、質問に答えましょう。

One of the research group members is currently working to elucidate how "plants communicate through strigolactones," hormones that hinder above-ground branching.

She said, "First, we want to find out how plants use strigolactones as a tool for predicting the future and understanding the presence of neighboring plants, and prove how smart they are."

(The Mainichi)

 Notes elucidate...「〜を解明する」 hinder...「〜を抑制する」

Which of the following is true about the research group members?

a. They are now trying to understand how a certain hormone is produced by plants.

b. According to one of the members, strigolactones play a role in communication among plants.

c. They hope that people will be able to use the plant hormone to predict the future.

d. They want to understand how plants communicate using their roots.

⊚ 10 Japan-led team finds plants may be using hormones to communicate, control growth

IMABARI, Ehime — A research group led by an Ehime University associate professor has shown that plants may use hormones to communicate beneath the soil and control their growth above it when they sense the presence of neighboring plants.

5 The team's findings have been published in the American scientific journal *Current Biology*.

"Plant hormone" is a general term for compounds produced by plants that boost or prevent growth, germination and flowering. The group consisting of researchers at Ehime University, Utsunomiya
10 University, and the University of Leeds in Britain focused on strigolactones, hormones that hinder above-ground branching. Strigolactones are chemically unstable and thus fragile, and can only be found in the soil near living roots.

The group first confirmed that the concentration of strigolactone
15 did not change whether they grew one or three rice plants in the same hydroponic culture solution. Researchers then found that as the number of rice plants was increased, the amount of strigolactone secreted per individual plant decreased, maintaining the same overall level of the hormone in the hydroponic environment.

20 When researchers doubled the amount of hydroponic solution without changing the number of rice plants, the plants secreted double the amount of strigolactone, again keeping the hormone's concentration constant.

The group then engineered two sets of rice plants not to secrete
25 strigolactone, one set that could absorb the hormone from the environment and the other that could not, and cultivated these together with wild rice plants. The first set of mutant plants actively absorbed strigolactone secreted by the wild rice plants, suppressing the excess branching caused by their own lack of the hormone.
30 Meanwhile, the second set kept over-branching despite being grown next to the wild plants.

(*The Mainichi* 一部抜粋・改変)

unstable「不安定な」
fragile「壊れやすい」

concentration「濃度」

hydroponic culture solution「水耕培養液」

secrete...「～を分泌する」

engineer...「～を操作する」

cultivate...「～を栽培する」
mutant「突然変異の」

suppress...「～を抑制する」

Comprehension

Choose two statements that are true about the passage.

1. Plants may use hormones to control their growth when sensing the presence of neighboring plants.
2. Strigolactones can be found anywhere in the soil.
3. When the researchers doubled the number of rice plants, the plants secreted double the amount of strigolactone.
4. The group engineered two sets of rice plants not to secrete strigolactone for their experiment.
5. The two sets of rice plants are the one that could absorb the hormone from the environment and the other that could not produce the hormone.

Summary

以下は本文の要約文です。1～4の空所に当てはまる語句を、選択肢から選び、書き入れましょう。

According to a research group (1.　　　　　　　　) by an Ehime University associate professor, plants may use hormones to communicate under the soil and control their growth when they sense the presence of (2.　　　　　　　) plants. The group focused on strigolactones, hormones that prevent plants from (3.　　　　　　). As the number of rice plants was increased, the amount of strigolactone secreted per individual plant decreased, (4.　　　　　　) the same amount of the hormone in the hydroponic environment.

maintaining	neighboring	led	branching

最新コインランドリー事情

Warm-up
1

音声を聴いて、グラフ（コインランドリーと共働き世帯の数の推移）を説明している英文を a ～ d から選びましょう。

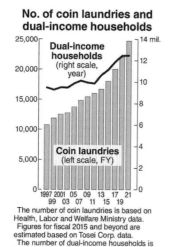

No. of coin laundries and dual-income households

Dual-income households (right scale, year)

Coin laundries (left scale, FY)

1997 2001 05 09 13 17 21
99 03 07 11 15 19

The number of coin laundries is based on Health, Labor and Welfare Ministry data. Figures for fiscal 2015 and beyond are estimated based on Tosei Corp. data.
The number of dual-income households is based on Internal Affairs and Communications Ministry data.

a. ☐

b. ☐

c. ☐

d. ☐

Warm-up
2

連なる 2 語の語尾と語頭が同じ音の場合、エリジョン（elision: 脱落）という現象が起こります。音が抜け落ちたり、2 倍の長さに発音されたりします。日本語を参考に、（　　）内に当てはまる語を書き入れましょう。その後、音声を聴いて答えを確認し、エリジョンに注意をして全文を読んでみましょう。

1. (　　　　　　　)(　　　　　　　　) competition among laundromats fierce, they are evolving to provide a wider array of services.

競争が激化する中、コインランドリーはより幅広いサービスを提供するために進化している。

2. Customers can (　　　　　　　)(　　　　　　　　) and futon covers by using special washing machines.

お客は、専用洗濯機を使って、シーツや布団カバーを洗うことができる。

3. Customers are free to visit (　　　　　　　)(　　　　　　　　) eat or drink, and on weekends the place bustles with families.

お客は、飲食だけのために訪れるのも自由で、週末は家族連れでにぎわう。

音声を聴いて、多くのコインランドリーに設置されている多機能洗濯機ができることとして、述べられているものを、1 ～ 4 から選びましょう。

1. ペット用マットの洗濯
2. 衣類のしみ抜き
3. 寝具のダニ退治
4. 寝具の消臭

以下の英文を読み、質問に答えましょう。

According to the Health, Labor and Welfare Ministry, the number of coin laundries has almost doubled in the past 20 years from 10,000 or so nationwide in fiscal 1997. Last fiscal year, the number is estimated to have exceeded 24,000. Behind this rise is an increase in the number of dual-income households.

"More and more households that are busy with work and child-rearing are washing clothes in batches on weekends to shorten the time for household chores," said an official of a coin laundry equipment manufacturer.

(The Japan News)

 Notes the Health, Labor and Welfare Ministry 「厚生労働省」 in batches 「まとめて」

Which of the following is mentioned in the passage?

a. The number of laundromats has increased by 10,000 over the past two decades.
b. It is estimated that the number of laundromats will exceed 24,000 next year.
c. Household washing machines have greatly reduced the burden of household chores.
d. More and more households are washing their laundry in bulk on weekends.

Coin laundries evolve to serve families

Coin laundries have been multiplying, especially in urban areas, and many now offer customers not only special washing machines but also a place to relax.

The number of coin laundries has doubled in the past 20 years
5 as more and more dual-income households use them to shorten the time spent on household chores. With the competition now fierce, the laundries are evolving to provide a wider array of services, such as cafes where customers can relax while waiting for their laundry to finish and specialized machines capable of washing shoes and futons.

10 Baluco Laundry Place Yoyogi-Uehara in Shibuya Ward, Tokyo, features its own cafe. Customers are free to visit just to eat or drink, and on weekends the place bustles with families.

"My husband and I both work, and since we have children, I have to run the washing machine many times at home," said a 45-year-
15 old woman doctor living in the neighborhood, who visited the coin laundry for the first time on Aug. 20. "Here, I can wash sheets and futon covers all at once. The atmosphere is cheerful, and it's nice to be able to spend my time in my own way at the cafe while doing laundry."

20 Okulab Inc., a Tokyo-based company that operates Baluco Laundry Place outlets, has six cafe-equipped laundries scattered across Tokyo, Kanagawa Prefecture and other prefectures. One of these laundries, located in the city of Kawasaki, has a sports club, too. "We want people to experience the convenience of doing laundry in a
25 short time, and what it's like to effectively use one's waiting time," an Okulab official said.

In the past, most coin laundries were used by single men and students, but in the past 10 years, an increasing number of coin laundries have targeted female customers. In addition to laundries
30 with cafes, some coin laundries have located themselves on the premises of shopping centers so that customers can go shopping while waiting.

(*The Japan News* 一部抜粋・改変)

multiply「増殖する」

feature...「～を特徴とする」

scatter...「～を展開する」

in addition to...「～に加えて」

premises「敷地」

26

Comprehension

Choose two statements that are true about the passage.

1. Some laundromats are equipped with special washing machines that can wash shoes.
2. The number of coin laundries has decreased by half in the last two decades.
3. A laundromat in Shibuya Ward, Tokyo, has a cafe in it.
4. A laundromat in Kawasaki City is exclusively for female customers.
5. The number of laundromats targeting male customers has been increasing these days.

Summary

以下は本文の要約文です。1〜4の空所に当てはまる語を、最初の1文字をヒントにして書き入れましょう。

In recent years, the number of laundromats has (1. i_____), offering a variety of services. Some are introducing specialized (2. m_____) with functions not available with home-use units. Some laundries with (3. c_____) allow customers to make effective use of their laundry time. Especially dual-income (4. h_____) can save time spent on household chores while enjoying cafe time there.

ゴキブリが人命救助？

Warm-up
1

音声を聴いて、写真（生きたマダガスカルゴキブリにさまざまな装置を装着して作製したサイボーグ昆虫）を説明している英文をa〜dから選びましょう。

写真提供：Reuters

a. ☐

b. ☐

c. ☐

d. ☐

Warm-up
2

名詞の複数語尾 (-s) は、名詞の語尾が有声音の場合は /z/、無声音の場合は /s/ と発音されます。ただし、語尾が (-t)(-d) のときは、/ts//dz/ となり一音として発音されます。また語尾 (-es) は /iz/ となります。日本語を参考に、音声を聴いて（　　）内に当てはまる名詞の複数形を書き入れましょう。その後、複数語尾の発音に注意をして全文を読んでみましょう。

1. The first responders to locate (　　　　　　　　) could be swarms of cyborg
(　　　　　　　).

生存者を見つけるのに最初に対応するものは、サイボーグゴキブリの群れかもしれない。

2. Cyborg (　　　　　　　) can enter hazardous (　　　　　　　) much more
efficiently than (　　　　　　　).

サイボーグ昆虫は、ロボットよりもはるかに効率良く危険区域に侵入できる。

3. The (　　　　　　　) can right (　　　　　　　) when flipped over.

それらの昆虫は、ひっくり返されたときに自力でもとの姿勢に戻ることができる。

音声を聴いて、ある実証実験におけるサイボーグゴキブリの動きについて<u>述べられ</u><u>ていないもの</u>はどれか、1 ～ 4 から選びましょう。

1. 動きは無線信号で指示された。
2. すべての指示に正確に反応した。
3. 左折の信号に応じて左折した。
4. 右折の信号に対して円を描くように動いた。

  以下の英文（サイボーグゴキブリに搭載する超薄型太陽電池）を読み、質問に答えましょう。

　　Beyond disaster rescue cockroaches, a researcher sees broad applications for the solar cell film used for the bugs. The film, composed of microscopic layers of plastic, silver and gold, could be built into clothing or skin patches for use in monitoring vital signs. On a sunny day, a parasol covered with the material could generate enough electricity to charge a mobile phone.

(The Japan News)

 be composed of...「～から構成されてる」　**microscopic**「微小な」

Which of the following is NOT true about the solar cell film?

a. It can be used for disaster rescue cockroaches.
b. It is composed of both metallic and non-metallic materials.
c. Clothing with it could measure vital signs.
d. Mobile phones covered with it will be developed.

🔊 20 Japan's cyber cockroach could prove boon in disaster-hit areas

SAITAMA (Reuters) — If an earthquake strikes in the not-too-distant future and survivors are trapped under tons of rubble, the first responders to locate them could be swarms of cyborg cockroaches.

That is a potential application of a recent breakthrough by
5 Japanese researchers who demonstrated the ability to mount "backpacks" of solar cells and electronics on the bugs and control their motion by remote control.

Kenjiro Fukuda and his team at the Thin-Film Device Laboratory at Japanese research giant Riken developed a flexible solar cell film
10 that is 4 microns thick, about 1/25 the width of a human hair, and can fit on the insect's abdomen.

The film allows the roach to move freely while the solar cell generates enough power to process and send directional signals into sensory organs on the bug's hindquarters.

15 The work builds upon previous insect-control experiments at Nanyang Technological University in Singapore and could one day result in cyborg insects that can enter hazardous areas much more efficiently than robots.

"The batteries inside small robots run out quickly, so the time for
20 exploration becomes shorter," Fukuda said. "A key benefit of a cyborg insect is that when it comes to an insect's movements, the insect is causing itself to move, so the electricity required is nowhere near as much."

Fukuda and his team chose Madagascar hissing cockroaches for
25 the experiments because they are big enough to carry the equipment and have no wings that would get in the way. Even when the backpack and film are glued to their backs, the bugs can traverse small obstacles or right themselves when flipped over.

The backpack and film can be removed, allowing the roaches
30 to go back to life in the lab's terrarium. The insects mature in four months and have been known to live up to five years in captivity.

(*The Japan News* 一部抜粋・改変)

Notes

boon「役立つもの」

trap...「～を閉じ込める」
tons of rubble「多量の瓦礫」

breakthrough「飛躍的な発明」

the Thin-Film Device Laboratory「薄膜デバイス研究所」

abdomen「腹部」

directional「方向指示の」

sensory organ「感覚器官」
hindquarter「後半身部」
previous「以前の」

exploration「探索」

when it comes to...「～に関して言えば」
nowhere near as much「ほとんどない」

get in the way「邪魔をする」
traverse...「～を越えていく」

terrarium「飼育器」
mature「成熟する」
in captivity「飼育下で」

Comprehension

Choose two statements that are true about the passage.

1. The backpack carried by a cockroach contains electronic devices.
2. The solar cell film mounted on a cockroach is thinner than a human hair.
3. The experiment conducted in Singapore was based on Fukuda's experiment.
4. The solar cell film cannot supply enough power to control a cockroach.
5. The cockroach used in Fukuda's experiment took four months to return to its normal life.

Summary

以下は本文の要約文です。1〜4の空所に当てはまる語句を、選択肢から選び、書き入れましょう。

A team of researchers has developed a "cyborg cockroach," a (1.　　　　　　　　) cockroach carrying a solar cell film and electronic devices on its back. The bug can be remotely controlled by (2.　　　　　　　) signals. As the cyborg insect can move by itself, it requires (3.　　　　　　　) electricity than a small robot. The researchers expect that the cyber cockroach could be used to search for survivors in (4.　　　　　　　) areas in the near future.

| live | disaster-hit | less | radio |

Nanyang Technological University

「即レス」時代に「亀レス」

 21
009

 Warm-up **1**

音声を聴いて、写真（文通サービスの会社「文通村」を経営している保科直樹氏が、最近事務局に届いた手紙に囲まれている）を説明している英文を a ～ d から選びましょう。

a. ☐

b. ☐

c. ☐

d. ☐

22
010

Warm-up **2**

-ing の ng は、「ング」という 2 音ではなく、/ŋ/ という発音記号で表される 1 音で発音します。舌の後面を口の中の天井奥の部分につけたまま鼻から息を出す鼻音です。日本語を参考に、音声を聴いて（　　）内に当てはまる語を書き入れましょう。その後、-ing の発音に注意をして全文を読んでみましょう。

1. Some people in Japan are (　　　　　　　　　) the warmth of people in old-fashioned correspondence.

   日本で、昔ながらの文通に人の温かさを見つけている人もいる。

2. While (　　　　　　) users' personal information secret, intermediary services allow them to correspond with their pen pals.

   個人情報を伏せたままで、仲介サービスによって、ユーザーはペンフレンドと文通をすることができる。

3. There are no risks of users' personal information (　　　　　　　　　) known to their pen pals.

   ユーザーの個人情報がペンフレンドに知られる恐れはない。

Warm-up 3A

音声（文通村のサービスについて）を聴いて、1 〜 5の空所内に適当な数字を書き入れましょう。

文通村のサービスの月額利用料は、税別で（1.　　　　）円から（2.　　　　）円、ドルに換算すると約（3.　　　　）ドルから（4.　　　　）ドルである。これまで文通村の事務局が仲介した手紙の総数は約（5.　　　　）通にのぼる。

Warm-up 3B

以下の英文を読み、質問に答えましょう。

　　Under Buntsumura's service, users only need to register their residential address via the service's website or by phone, before they are allocated fictitious "addresses" they can use in their correspondence. They then look for potential pen pals on the website and, if they find one they like, they send a letter to the secretariat with the assigned address and a pseudonym. The secretariat forwards the letter to the residence of the addressee.

(The Mainichi)

Notes allocate.../assign... 「〜を割り当てる」　pseudonym 「仮名」　forward... 「〜を転送する」　addressee 「受取人」

Which of the following is true about the passage?

a. Users must register their real name and residential address.

b. Users correspond with a person introduced by the secretariat.

c. Users send letters directly to their pen pals under a temporary name.

d. The secretariat exchanges letters on behalf of users.

25 Why are some people in Japan finding solace in old-fashioned correspondence?

TOKYO — In this age of fast-moving social media, some people in Japan are turning to old-fashioned correspondence with pen pals, apparently because handwritten letters can bring the hearts of senders closer to recipients. Services allowing people to correspond
5 with others while keeping their real names, residential addresses, and other personal information secret are also growing. The Mainichi Shimbun explored what is behind the renewed spotlight on longhand correspondence.

Until around a few decades ago, this kind of correspondence
10 was common. Magazines would have correspondence sections, filled with the addresses of those looking for pen pals. However, with the enactment of the Act on the Protection of Personal Information in Japan in 2003, stricter rules were applied for the handling of personal information. With the spread of the internet, correspondence sections
15 in magazines vanished one after the other.

Then came the advent of intermediary services for those who prefer to correspond without revealing their names and residential addresses.

Naoki Hoshina, 39, of Narita, Chiba Prefecture, launched
20 Buntsumura, a service allowing users to exchange letters while keeping their personal data secret, in 2009.

There are no risks of users' real names, home addresses or other personal information being known to their pen pals. As the fictitious addresses are named after figures and specialties in each of Japan's
25 47 prefectures, such as "Shingen street" (in reference to 16th century warlord Takeda Shingen) and "Momiji Manju-dori avenue" (referring to a popular sweet in Hiroshima Prefecture), senders can assume which prefecture their pen pals reside in, allowing both ends of correspondence to talk about local topics unique to the area.

30 "I've been able to come in contact with the warmth of people. Though email and social media are now mainstream in society, I once again found exchanging letters valuable," a letter sent to the secretariat read.

(*The Mainichi* 一部抜粋・改変)

solace「癒し」

turn to...「～を始める」
apparently「どうも～らしい」

explore...「～を探る」
longhand「手書き」

enactment「施行」
handling「取り扱い」

vanish「消え去る」

advent「登場」
intermediary「仲介の」
reveal...「～を明かす」

figure「人物」
specialty「名産品」

assume...「～を想定する」
reside in...「～に住む」

Comprehension

Choose two statements that are true about the passage.

1. Social media can convey senders' messages swiftly and accurately.
2. Social media is safe because its users can exchange messages without revealing their personal information.
3. Some magazines have correspondence sections even now.
4. Hoshina provides a service that allows users to exchange letters with keeping their personal information secret.
5. Users of Hoshina's service communicate using pseudonyms and fictitious addresses.

Summary

以下は本文の要約文です。１〜４の空所に当てはまる語を、最初の一文字をヒントにして書き入れましょう。

Now that communication via the (1. i   ) has become mainstream, some people have started correspondence with pen pals to exchange (2. l   ), because they feel the warmth of people through letters. Since strict rules have been applied for the handling of (3. p   ) information, intermediary services have emerged to meet the needs of those who wish to keep their home addresses, real names, and other personal information (4. s   ).

医療・社会

薬もバーチャルサービスで

26
011

Warm-up **1**

音声を聴いて、写真（オンラインで患者とやりとりしている薬剤師）を説明している英文をa～dから選びましょう。

a. ☐

b. ☐

c. ☐

d. ☐

27
012

Warm-up **2**

/s/ と /ʃ/ はまったく異なる発音です。/ʃ/ は静かにしてほしいときに「シーっ」と言うときの音に近く発音されますが、一方、/s/ は「ス」のように発音されます。日本語を参考に、音声を聴いて（　　）内に当てはまる語を書き入れましょう。その後、/s/ と /ʃ/ の発音に注意をして全文を読んでみましょう。

1. (　　　　　　　　　) can speak with (　　　　　　　　　) online and ask them about how to take their medications.

患者は薬剤師とオンラインで話をして、薬の飲み方について尋ねることができる。

2. A 58-year-old woman wanted to avoid being outside for long periods due to her compromised immune (　　　　　　　).

58歳の女性は免疫不全のため長時間の外出を避けたいと思っていた。

3. Nihon Chouzai Co. has been providing virtual medication administration instructions (　　　　　　　) September 2020.

日本調剤株式会社は、2020年9月よりヴァーチャルでの投薬管理の指導を提供してきた。

音声を聴いて、ある医師の意見によると、オンラインの調剤サービスは、どのような人に便利だと述べられているか、1 ～ 5 から 2 つ選びましょう。

1. 忙しい人
2. 感染を恐れる人
3. じっくり相談したい人
4. 早く薬が欲しい人
5. 対面販売が苦手な人

以下の英文（薬剤師とオンラインで相談できるサービスついて）を読み、質問に答えましょう。

Previously, online pharmacist consultation services were only allowed for virtual medical examinations or examinations at home, and only if the first consultation was done in person. In March, however, the Health, Labor and Welfare Ministry allowed online consultations for prescription administration instructions, including the first consultation depending on the pharmacist's approval, regardless of how a patient receives medical care.

(The Japan News)

 in person「対面で」 **approval**「承認」

Which of the following is NOT true about online pharmacist consultation?

a. The online consultation services were already allowed by the Welfare Ministry earlier for limited cases.

b. There were already online medical examination services.

c. Patients could receive the pharmacist consultation service online after they consulted a pharmacist in person.

d. After the approval by the Welfare Ministry, to use the online consultation services, patients need to visit a pharmacy first.

30

Online pharmacies offer easier patient consultations

The service of pharmacists being able to speak with patients online and provide them with instructions on how to take their prescriptions has been gaining attention as patients can now receive their medications through the mail. The virtual service is popular among those who want to avoid going outside as a result of the pandemic or who do not have time to go to the pharmacy.

A 58-year-old Saitama woman who suffers from rheumatism has been using the service since the spring. She visits a hospital two hours away and used to pick up her prescription at a pharmacy near there. The medicine must be refrigerated, and the ice packs are heavy. She also wanted to avoid being outside for long periods due to her compromised immune system.

"At the pharmacy, I'm aware of the people behind me who are waiting, but at home, I can ask the pharmacist questions without worrying about that," she said. "Since my prescription is sent to my house, I don't have to bring back a lot of medications, so that's also convenient."

Tokyo-based dispensing pharmacy company Nihon Chouzai Co. has been providing virtual medication administration instructions since September 2020. After seeing a doctor at a hospital, patients reserve a time slot to speak to a pharmacist online to receive an explanation on how to take their medications. Prescriptions are delivered from hospitals to pharmacies.

Ain Holdings Inc., the Hokkaido-based operator of Ain pharmacies, has been providing the virtual service since 2020 as well. In February, the company launched a texting chat service in which patients can easily ask their questions to a pharmacist.

There are services that allow patients to receive medical care, receive explanations of medicines, and have them delivered, the process of which can all be done through their smartphones.

Patients sign up through apps such as "Sokuyaku" and "Clinics," and make an appointment. Medical examinations, medication consultations, deliveries and payments are all handled through such apps.

prescription 「処方薬」

rheumatis 「リウマチ」

refrigerate... 「〜を冷蔵する」

dispensing pharmacy company 「調剤薬局会社」

time slot 「時間枠」

(*The Japan News* 一部抜粋・改変)

Comprehension

Choose two statements that are true about the passage.

1. In the new online services, pharmacists provide customers with advice on how to take medications.
2. All the prescriptions ordered online are received at a nearby pharmacy.
3. Patients have to prepare questions that they want to ask a pharmacist before consultation.
4. A Hokkaido-based pharmacy operator started a texting chat service in 2020.
5. Apps such as "Sokuyaku" and "Clinics"are now popular among people.

Summary

以下は本文の要約文です。1～4の空所に当てはまる語句を、選択肢から選び、書き入れましょう。

The online pharmacist consultation service has been gaining (1.　　　　　　　). Patients can speak with a pharmacist online and receive instructions about how to take medications. They can also get the (2.　　　　　　) delivered. It is convenient for those who want to avoid going outside due to the pandemic or who do not have time to go to the (3.　　　　　　). There are other services using apps such as "Sokuyaku" and "Clinics." Medical examinations, medication (4.　　　　　　), deliveries and payments are all handled through these apps.

pharmacy consultations prescriptions attention

忙しいときの助っ人

 31
013

Warm-up 1　音声を聴いて、写真（完全栄養食品）を説明している英文を a 〜 d から選びましょう。

a. ☐

b. ☐

c. ☐

d. ☐

32
014

Warm-up 2　/b/ と /v/ は、同じ音としてカタカナ表記されることがありますが、まったく異なる音です。/b/ は、閉じた両唇のすき間から息をはじき出す感じで発音します。一方、/v/ は、上前歯を軽く下唇に当てたまま息を吐き出します。日本語を参考に、（　　　）内に当てはまる語を書き入れましょう。その後、音声を聴いて答えを確認し、全文を読んでみましょう。

1. The company (　　　　　　　　　) more than 10 ingredients, including soybeans and kombu, into a whole-grain (　　　　　　).

その会社は、大豆や昆布など 10 種類以上の素材をブレンドし、全粒粉ベースにしている。

2. Three to four times a week for (　　　　　　　), she eats (　　　　　　　) that claims to (　　　　　) a complete nutritional food.

彼女は、週に 3 〜 4 回、朝食に完全栄養食品と謳われているパンを食べている。

3. She can eat the complete nutritional food every day (　　　　　　) it has a wide (　　　　　　) of flavors and types.

彼女は、その完全栄養食品は味も種類も豊富なので、毎日でも食べることができる。

Warm-up 3A

音声（厚生労働省の「日本人の食事摂取基準」ガイドラインに沿って、完全栄養食を開発している食品会社の関係者のコメント）を聴いて、製品について関係者が<u>述べていないこと</u>を、1〜4から選びましょう。

1. 33 種類の栄養素が含まれている。
2. 厚生労働省のガイドラインに沿っている。
3. 栄養的にバランスが取れている。
4. 健康志向の人向けである。

Warm-up 3B

以下の英文を読み、質問に答えましょう。

　　Solid-type nutritional supplements have been available for more than 30 years, but the first product marketed as a complete nutritional meal is said to be Soylent, from a U.S. startup, about 10 years ago. Since then, the trend toward simplified meals and health consciousness has continued to grow.

　　KBV Research, a global market research and consulting company with bases in the United States and other countries, estimates that the global market for complete nutritional foods will grow at an average annual rate of 6.5% from 2021 and will expand to $6.3 billion by 2027.

(The Japan News)

 Notes startup「スタートアップ企業」 estimate...「〜と推定する」 expand「拡大する」

Which of the following is true about complete nutritional foods?

a. The first complete nutritional meal was introduced approximately three decades ago.

b. Soylent was a complete nutritional food developed by a well-established U.S. company.

c. KBV Research is a company that sells various types of complete nutritional foods.

d. According to KBV Research, the market for complete nutrition foods is expected to expand significantly.

35 # 'Complete' foods claim to supply daily nutrients

Can consuming "complete nutritional foods" provide all the nutrients necessary for daily life, as these products claim?

These foods have traditionally been beverage-type products, but drawing attention these days are products such as bread and instant
5 noodles that offer more options for people who do not eat three square meals.

Most domestic products seem to be made in consideration of the standard intake of 33 nutrients, including vitamins, minerals, carbohydrates, proteins and fats, as indicated in the "Dietary
10 Reference Intakes for Japanese" guideline published by the health ministry.

Three to four times a week for breakfast, a 21-year-old female college student living in Kanagawa Prefecture eats bread that claims to be a complete nutritional food.

15 "It's difficult to prepare a well-balanced meal in the morning," she said. "I can eat this bread every day because it has a wide variety of flavors and types."

The bread she eats is made by Base Food, Inc., which was established in 2016. In addition to bread, the company has developed
20 pasta and cookies in its range of complete nutritional food. The company blends more than 10 ingredients, including soybeans and kombu, into a whole-grain base, and one serving provides more than one-third of the nutrients in the standard daily dietary intake.

Base Food Chief Executive Officer Shun Hashimoto said he had
25 wanted to end his habit of eating out, but had been unsuccessful in his attempts to cook for himself.

"For busy working people, it is difficult to keep cooking several healthy dishes per meal," he said. "Bread and noodles make it easy to keep up with healthy eating."

(*The Japan News* 一部抜粋・改変)

nutrient「栄養素」

beverage「飲料」

option「選択肢」
three square meals「日に3食」

domestic「国内の」

intake「摂取量」

carbohydrate「炭水化物」
indicate...「〜を示す」

serving「食」

Comprehension

Choose two statements that are true about the passage.

1. Complete nutritional foods can be solid or beverage type.
2. Complete nutritional foods are suitable for people who eat three meals a day.
3. Complete nutritional foods are produced according to companies' own guidelines.
4. A female college student sometimes eats three to four meals per day.
5. Mr. Hashimoto had been unsuccessful in his attempts to cook for himself.

Summary

以下は本文の要約文です。1〜4の空所に当てはまる語を、最初の一文字をヒントにして書き入れましょう。

Complete nutritional foods are now a great help to (1. b   ) people. Not only do they save (2. t   ), but they also eliminate the hassle of cooking one's own food. Many companies' products contain 33 different (3. n   ), in line with the Ministry of Health and Welfare's guidelines, making the foods an option for (4. h   )-conscious people in their daily diet.

食事バランスガイド（厚生労働省 HP より）

SDGs: ある企業の取り組み

36
015

Warm-up
1

音声を聴いて、写真（廃材利用の「残材 BANK」プロジェクト」に取り組んでいる中美建設の代表取締役、中村淳二氏）を説明している英文をa ～ d から選びましょう。

a. ☐

b. ☐

c. ☐

d. ☐

37
016

Warm-up
2

連なる 2 語の語尾と語頭が同音ではなくても、発音する際の口の形や舌の位置がほぼ同じの場合、chapter 3 で取り上げたエリジョン（elision: 脱落）という現象が起こります。音声を聴いて（　　　）内に当てはまる語を書き入れましょう。その後、エリジョンに注意をして全文を読んでみましょう。

1. The Zanzai Bank is (　　　　　　　　) to promote the reuse of scrap wood.

   残材バンクは、廃材の再利用を促進することを目的としている。

2. The company is not (　　　　　　　　) to burn scrap wood, a common former practice in the industry.

   その業者は、業界ではかつて一般的なやり方であった廃材の焼却は許可されていない。

3. What a local (　　　　　　　　) contractor can do may be small, but we can make a difference when we work together.

   地元の建設業者ができることは小さいかもしれないが、協力し合えば大きな力になる。

音声を聴いて、「残材 BANK」を利用した女性について述べられているものはどれか、1 〜 4 から選びましょう。

1. 年齢は 17 歳で、地元の女性である。
2. 手に入れるつもりの残材は無料である。
3. 建設予定の長男の自宅に残材を利用しようと思った。
4. 手に入れた残材で、植木鉢を自作することにしていた。

以下の英文（三重県伊勢市にある中美建設が行っている残材 BANK 利用手続きについて）を読み、質問に答えましょう。

Ise-based Nakayoshi Corp. started the Zanzai Bank to offer scrap lumber. The company posts photos of the leftover wood on its Instagram account (@zanzaibank_ise) and also lets people know a time frame to come to pick it up.

It tells anyone willing to pick up the wood to visit the garden at Middle Earth Village, a furniture and daily goods shop that opened near its main office in June, to pick it up.

(The Asahi Shimbun)

 post...「〜を投稿する」 **leftover wood**「残材」

Which of the following does a person who wants leftover wood have to do?

a. To negotiate with Nakayoshi Corp. about its price
b. To tell Nakayoshi Corp. of the desired pick-up date
c. To go to the garden at Middle Earth Village to pick it up
d. To pay a pick-up fee to Middle Earth Village

Reading

◉ 40 Housebuilders start up 'wood banks' to reuse scrap lumber

ISE, Mie Prefecture — A local construction company has launched a new effort through social media to give away its leftover lumber from building houses for free.

It is part of a fledgling nationwide recycling trend that benefits
5 homebuilders, hobbyists and the environment all at the same time by eliminating costs and reducing construction material waste.

Dubbed "Zanzai Bank" (bank for remainder materials), the project is designed to promote the reuse of scrap wood while catering to increased demand from do-it-yourself enthusiasts.

10 Other similar efforts are becoming widespread among small and midsize firms across the country, the company said.

Ise-based Nakayoshi Corp. started the Zanzai Bank to offer scrap lumber from locally grown "hinoki" cypress and cedar trees ranging in length from 50 to 150 centimeters.

15 According to President Junji Nakamura, 44, the company mostly builds houses. The pillars and other building materials it uses are processed at a factory before they are carried into construction sites. But the company brings in extra materials for the ceiling and other structures to be cut on site, which creates wood waste. About six
20 cubic meters of scrap wood is produced from one house, he said.

The company is not allowed to burn the scrap wood, a common former practice in the industry, and Nakayoshi has had to pay a waste removal company to haul away most of the excess wood in the past.

When the president was researching ways to reuse the wood,
25 he was encouraged by an acquaintance at the Kanazawa-based construction firm Iemoto, which launched its own Zanzai Bank in June last year, to follow suit. Nakayoshi said they have received many requests so far.

"What a local building contractor can do may be small, but we
30 can make a difference when we work together," he said. "It also contributes to the U.N. Sustainable Development Goals (SDGs)."

(*The Asahi Shimbun* 一部抜粋・改変)

Notes:
housebuilder「住宅建設業者」
launch...「～を始める」
give away...「～を譲る」
fledgling「始まったばかりの」
benefit...「～に利益をもたらす」
eliminate...「～を削減する」
dub...「～と称する」
cater to...「～に応える」
enthusiast「愛好家」
cedar「スギ」
pillar「柱」
process...「～を加工する」
haul away...「～を撤去する」
excess「余分な」
acquaintance「知人」
follow suit「先例に従う」

Comprehension

Choose two statements that are true about the passage.

1. Nakayoshi Corp. uses leftover materials for building its own office.
2. Zanzai Bank is a project launched by local governments across Japan.
3. Leftover materials are not widely used by DIY enthusiasts.
4. Nakayoshi Corp. processes building materials such as pillars at a factory.
5. Nakamura's Zanzai Bank was inspired by the efforts of Iemoto.

Summary

以下は本文の要約文です。1～4の空所に当てはまる前置詞を、選択肢の中から選び、空所内に書き入れましょう。

As part of the United Nations Sustainable Development Goals, Zanzai Bank projects have been launched (1. _____) the country in an attempt to reuse waste wood (2. _____) home construction. These environmentally-friendly projects, promoted (3. _____) small and medium-sized home builders, are expected to create a win-win relationship (4. _____) home builders and DIY enthusiasts.

between	throughout	from	by

「不便」がヒントに

Warm-up 1

音声を聴いて、写真（佐藤美恵子さんと、彼女が発明した「ペットボトル開けるくん」）を説明している英文を a ～ d から選びましょう。

a. ☐

b. ☐

c. ☐

d. ☐

Warm-up 2

不定冠詞 a（an）の直前の単語が子音で終わる場合はリンキングが起こり、音がつながって発音されます。音声を聴いて（　　）内に当てはまる語を書き入れましょう。その後、不定冠詞とのリンキングに注意をして全文を読んでみましょう。

1. An 89-year-old woman (　　　　　　　) a hit product that now sells tens of thousands of (　　　　　) a year.

   ある 89 歳の女性が、現在年間何万個も売れるヒット商品を作り出した。

2. The tool is made by hand by (　　　　　　　) a rubber tube into a 4-centimeter length, dyeing it, drilling holes in it, and (　　　　　) a string through it.

   その道具は手製で、ゴムのチューブを長さ 4 センチにカットし、染色し、ドリルで穴を開けて、ひもを通して作られている。

3. The inventor says (　　　　　　　) a smile, "I don't have time to die."

   その発明家は、「死んでいる暇はありません」と笑いながら言う。

Warm-up 3A

音声を聴いて、東京に本拠のある発明学会の会員の大半はどのような人たちか、述べられているものを 1 ～ 4 から選びましょう。

1. 発明家にアドバイスをする専門家
2. 元エンジニア
3. アマチュア発明家
4. 発明家希望の若者

Warm-up 3B

以下の英文（佐藤美恵子さんの発明秘話）を読み、質問に答えましょう。

The inspiration for the product came when Sato felt her strength waning as she began having difficulty unscrewing the caps of plastic bottles. The prototype, which was made with a flat rubber band, prevented the lid from slipping, allowing it to be opened without much effort.

After consulting with the Tokyo-based Hatsumei-gakkai, a general incorporated association that supports people who love inventions, Sato obtained a patent in 2011. She went through trial and error to finally commercialize the product in its current form, which is made from rubber tubing with a 2.8-centimeter diameter.

(The Mainichi)

 Notes wane「衰える」 unscrew...「～を開ける」 general incorporated association「一般社団法人」
obtain...「～を取得する」 patent「特許」 commercialize...「～を商品化する」

Which of the following is true about the story behind Sato's invention?

a. Sato has long wanted to invent something new for drinks in plastic bottles.

b. When making the prototype, she used rubber to prevent the cap from slipping.

c. Hatsumei-gakkai asked her to commercialize her product in 2011.

d. Her final form of the product has yet to be completed.

45 89-yr-old Tokyo woman continues to invent, inspired by problems she faces in daily life

face...「～に直面する」

TOKYO — An 89-year-old woman has shown that people do not necessarily need special knowledge or skills to start inventing — by creating a hit product that now sells tens of thousands of units a year.

5　Eleven years ago, Mieko Sato, a resident of Machida, Tokyo, created a tool to open plastic bottles using only a small amount of force. The rubber tool, named "Plastic bottle akeru-kun," is available at co-operative stores nationwide for 400 yen (about $3) per piece, and 30,000 to 40,000 of them are sold each year.

10　While she is now advanced in years, Sato says with a smile, "I don't have time to die."

The tool is made by hand by cutting a rubber tube into a 4-centimeter length, dyeing it, drilling holes in it, and threading a string through it.

thread ～ through...
「～を…に通す」

15　In 2013, when Sato and her fellow inventors exhibited their products at a department store event, the plastic bottle openers sold so fast that she had to rush to make additional ones. She sold 280 of them in five days, using up all the materials she had prepared. This spring, she received a monthly order for 5,000 units, and she and her
20　husband worked hard to fill it.

"All you need to invent something is motivation and the ability to take action as soon as you hit upon an idea," said Sato. "I don't have the academic background or the skills, but it doesn't matter. It's worth it, knowing that my products are helping someone." Her
25　approach indicates that the first step is to solve the inconveniences and problems people experience in their daily lives.

hit upon...「～を思いつく」

worth...「～の価値がある」

indicate...「～を示す」
inconvenience「不便さ」

Sato has also developed tools for opening jam jars and cans, and has recently been working to commercialize "zori slippers" – slippers with geta straps attached.

(*The Mainichi* 一部抜粋・改変)

Comprehension

Choose two statements that are true about the passage.

1. Sato's plastic bottle opener can be purchased at convenience stores.
2. The forty thousand units of the openers she has made have been sold so far.
3. It was at a department store that Sato first sold the product.
4. Sato thinks that it is important to take action soon after getting inspiration for an invention.
5. Sato suggests that expertise is essential for inventing something.

Summary

以下は本文の要約文です。1〜4の空所に当てはまる語句を、選択肢から選び、書き入れましょう。

An 89-year-old woman has invented some (1. _____) to solve problems in our daily life. One of her products is a tool to open plastic bottles without any (2. _____). The rubber tool is named "Plastic bottle akeru-kun," and is available at co-operative (3. _____) for 400 yen per piece. She has also developed tools for opening jam jars and cans. She hopes that her products will help people solve their daily (4. _____).

inconveniences	products	stores	effort

Chapter 10

月に住む：夢物語が現実に

46
019
Warm-up 1

音声を聴いて、イラスト（月に長期滞在をするのに必要なインフラの概念図）を説明している英文を a ～ d から選びましょう。

Research on infrastructure required for long-term lunar stays

Electricity, energy
Housing

Small nuclear reactor (NASA)
Lunar housing (Kajima Corp., others)

Travel
Other topics

Water-extraction technology, high-speed communication technology, etc.

Lunar exploration vehicle (JAXA, Toyota Motor Corp.)

写真提供：トヨタ自動車、NASA、
JAXA、鹿島建設

a. ☐

b. ☐

c. ☐

d. ☐

47
020
Warm-up 2

規則動詞の過去形語尾 (-ed) は、動詞の語尾が有声音の場合は /d/、無声音の場合は /t/ と発音されます。また、動詞の語尾が /d/ あるいは /t/ の場合は、/id/ と発音されます。日本語を参考に、音声を聴いて（　　）内に当てはまる動詞の過去形を書き入れましょう。その後、-ed の発音に注意をして全文を読んでみましょう。

1. NASA (　　　　　　　　) it had chosen three private companies to provide basic designs for a small nuclear reactor.

米国航空宇宙局（NASA）は、小型原子炉の基本設計を提供する民間企業 3 社を選定したと発表した。

2. NASA and Washington University will jointly build a rover-(　　　　　　　　) drill and a laser-(　　　　　　　　) monitoring device.

NASA とワシントン大学は、ローバーに搭載するドリルやレーザーによるモニタリング装置を共同で製作することになっている。

3. The (　　　　　　　　) facilities comprise a large glass-(　　　　　　　　) structure.

想定している施設は、巨大なグラスの形をした構造物からなる。

音声を聴いて、アルテミス計画（アメリカ主導の月面着陸計画）のために宇宙航空研究開発機構（JAXA）とトヨタ自動車が開発を進めているものはどれか、1 ～ 4 から選びましょう

1. 無人月面探査車
2. ルナ・クルーザーと呼ばれる月面基地
3. 宇宙服なしで運転できる月面探査車
4. 2 ～ 4 人乗りのソーラーカー

以下の英文を読み、質問に答えましょう。

The Artemis Program, which comprises multiple missions, aims to construct a moon-orbiting base by the late 2020s, and later, another base on the lunar surface.

Astronauts will be tasked with exploring the moon's surface, excavating its regolith and conducting various scientific experiments. Japan is one of eight partner countries participating in the mission and the government has set a goal of having a Japanese astronaut land on the moon by the late 2020s.

(The Japan News)

 orbit「周回する」 **explore...**「〜を探査する」 **excavate...**「〜を掘削する」 **regolith**「レゴリス：天体表面に堆積している砂」

Which of the following is NOT stated as the missions of astronauts participating in the Artemis Program?

a. To build a base on the moon
b. To explore the lunar surface
c. To dig in the lunar ground
d. To make a variety of experiments

Japan, U.S. rocketing ahead with lunar infrastructure plans

The U.S.-led Artemis Program is shooting for the moon. The international lunar exploration program has a broad range of objectives, including the return of humans to the surface of Earth's closest celestial neighbor for the first time since the Apollo 17
5　mission in 1972.

Research and development to install lunar infrastructure such as electricity, water and housing is currently in full swing in the United States and Japan, with the aim of building a habitable moon base that can facilitate long-term stays.

10　A stable supply of electricity is one of the major challenges facing long-term moon-based activities: It takes approximately 27 days for the moon to rotate once on its axis, so lunar days and lunar nights each last about two weeks. As such, electricity from solar power alone may not meet nighttime electricity demands.

15　The U.S. National Aeronautics and Space Administration (NASA) is currently eyeing nuclear power generation on the moon. In late June, NASA announced it had chosen three private companies to provide basic designs for a small nuclear reactor and would provide each firm with about $5 million (about ¥700 million).

20　Water is essential for life, and it is believed that the lunar regolith contains this life-sustaining compound. NASA and Washington University in St. Louis will jointly build a rover-mounted drill and a laser-based monitoring device to quantify the amount and distribution of water beneath the moon's surface.

25　Kyoto University and the major contractor Kajima Corp., meanwhile, have proposed housing facilities for lunar-based human habitation. The envisioned facilities comprise a large glass-shaped structure measuring 200 meters in diameter and 200 to 400 meters in height that can rotate to create a centrifugal force. This would allow
30　about 1,000 people to live in an environment with a similar level of gravity to that of the Earth, according to the university and the company.

(*The Japan News* 一部抜粋・改変)

shoot for...「〜を目指す」

objective「目的」
Earth's closest celestial neighbor「地球に最も近い天の隣人：月のこと」

be in full swing「本格化している」
habitable「居住可能な」

facilitate...「〜を容易にする」
stable「安定した」

axis「軸」

eye...「〜を視野に入れている、もくろむ」

compound「化合物」

quantify...「〜を定量化する」
distribution「分布」

contractor「建設業者」

centrifugal force「遠心力」

gravity「重力、引力」

Comprehension

Choose two statements that are true about the passage.

1. The Artemis Program aims to send humans to Mars.
2. About 50 years have passed since humans landed on the moon for the first time.
3. Private companies can participate in the Artemis Program by investing $5 million.
4. NASA and Washington University do not believe that water exists on the moon.
5. The envisioned housing facilities on the moon would accommodate approximately 1,000 people.

Summary

以下は本文の要約文です。１〜４の空所に当てはまる語を、最初の一文字をヒントにして書き入れましょう。

The U.S.-led "Artemis Program" is a research and development project based on the premise that (1. h　　　　　　) will be able to live on the moon for a long period of time. In order to realize this goal, (2. i　　　　　　) such as electricity, water, and housing must be prepared on the moon. Kyoto University and Kajima Corp. have already (3. p　　　　　　) the concept of housing facilities on the moon where about one (4. t　　　　　　) people can live.

悪者を守れ!

 51
021

Warm-up 1 音声を聴いて、写真（ニシレモンザメが他の魚と泳いでいる）を説明している英文をa〜dから選びましょう。

a.

b.

c.

d.

写真提供：AFP-jiji

52
022

Warm-up 2 前置詞がある場合、その前置詞の前後の単語の音がリンキングしてつながって聞こえることがあります。日本語を参考に、（　）内に当てはまる前置詞を書き入れましょう。その後、音声を聴いてつながって聞こえるところに下線を引き、全文を読んでみましょう。

1. Delegates approved a plan to protect many shark species (　　　　　) a global summit.

グローバルサミットで、代表者らは多くのサメの種を保護する計画を承認した。

2. Shirley Binder, Panamanian delegate and head (　　　　　) the plenary of the requiem shark proposal, said "Proposal 37 approved."

パナマの代表であり、メジロザメに関する提案の会議の議長を務めるシャーリー・バインダー氏は「提案37が承認されました」と述べた。

3. Sharks have long been seen (　　　　　) the villain of the seas they have occupied for more than 400 million years.

サメは長らく4億年以上もの間占領してきた海の悪者とみなされてきた。

音声を聴いて、絶滅が危惧されるサメについて述べられていないものはどれか、1
〜 4 から選びましょう。

1. 成熟するまでにかかる年数
2. 繁殖率の低さ
3. 個体数減少の原因
4. 獲物を狩る方法の多様さ

 Notes maturity「成熟」 fertility rate「繁殖率」

以下の英文（サメ（フカ）のヒレについて）を読み、質問に答えましょう。

　　Insatiable appetite in Asia for shark fins, which make their way onto dinner tables in Hong Kong, Taiwan and Japan, has spurred their trade. Despite being described as almost tasteless and gelatinous, shark fin soup is viewed as a delicacy and is enjoyed by the very wealthy, often at weddings and expensive banquets. Shark fins, representing a market of about $500 million per year, can sell for about $1,000 a kilogram.

(The Japan News, AFP-jiji)

Notes insatiable「飽くなき」 appetite「欲」 spur...「〜に拍車をかける」 gelatinous「ゼラチン状の」
delicacy「おいしいもの」 represent...「〜に相当する」

Which of the following is true about shark fins?

a. Some Asian countries crave shark fins.
b. Shark fin soup is enjoyed as an ordinary dish by wealthy people.
c. Shark fin soup is the most popular soup for expensive banquets.
d. Annual sales of shark fins are approximately $1,000.

Global wildlife summit approves shark protections

●55

PANAMA CITY (AFP-Jiji) — Delegates at a global summit on trade in endangered species on Nov. 25 approved a plan to protect 54 more shark species, a move that could drastically reduce the lucrative and cruel shark fin trade.

5　Members of the requiem shark and the hammerhead shark families will now have their trade tightly controlled under *the Convention on International Trade in Endangered Species (CITES).

"Proposal 37 approved," said Panamanian delegate and head of the plenary Shirley Binder of the requiem shark proposal, after 10　Japan failed in getting the blue shark removed from the measure. The proposal regarding the hammerhead shark passed without debate.

Binder earlier told AFP the "historic decision" would mean up to 90% of sharks in the market would now be protected.

"This will be remembered as the day we turned the tide to prevent 15　the extinction of the world's sharks and rays," said Luke Warwick, director of shark protection for the NGO **Wildlife Conservation Society (WCS).

The shark species will now be listed on what is known as CITES Appendix II, which is for species that may not yet be threatened 20　with extinction but may become so unless trade in them is closely controlled.

"The crucial next step will be to implement these listings, and ensure they result in stronger fisheries management and trade measures as soon as possible," Warwick said.

25　Sharks have long been seen as the villain of the seas they have occupied for more than 400 million years, drawing horror with their depiction in films such as "Jaws" and occasional attacks on humans.

However, these ancient predators have undergone an image makeover in recent years as conservationists have highlighted the 30　crucial role they play in regulating the ocean ecosystem.

Joaquin de la Torre of ***the International Fund for Animal Welfare (IFAW) told AFP that more than 100 million sharks are killed every year.

(The Japan News, AFP-jiji 一部抜粋・改変)

*　the Convention on International Trade in Endangered Species (CITES)「絶滅のおそれのある野生動植物の種の国際取引に関する条約」ワシントン条約のこと
**　Wildlife Conservation Society (WCS)「国際野生生物保全協会」科学的な調査に基づいた野生生物の保全活動や環境教育などを行っている
***　the International Fund for Animal Welfare (IFAW)「国際動物福祉基金」商業捕鯨反対運動や災害時の動物救助など動物の保護活動を行っている

Notes

drastically「大幅に」
lucrative「営利目的の」

hammerhead shark「シュモクザメ」

blue shark「ヨシキリザメ」
measure「提案」

turn the tide「流れを変える」
ray「エイ」

appendix「付属書」

implement...「〜を実行する」
ensure...「〜を確実にする」

depiction「描写」

predator「捕食者」
undergo an image makeover「イメージチェンジする」
regulate...「〜を調整する」

Choose two statements that are true about the passage.

1. Members of the requiem shark and the hammerhead shark families have their trade tightly controlled so far.
2. Shirley Binder opposed Proposal 37, but the proposal passed without debate.
3. It is necessary to take stronger measures for fisheries management and their trade as soon as possible.
4. People have been scared of sharks for a long time.
5. In spite of conservationists' campaigns, sharks have gained no good reputation.

Summary

以下は本文の要約文です。1～4の空所に当てはまる語を、選択肢から選び、書き入れましょう

A plan to protect 54 more shark species was (1.   ) at a global summit on trade in (2.   ) species. Panamanian delegate Shirley Binder called this a "historic decision" and up to 90% of sharks in the market will now be (3.   ). Japan failed in getting the blue shark removed from the proposal. The species will now be considered as that which may not yet be (4.   ) with extinction but may become so unless trade in them is severely controlled.

protected	endangered	approved	threatened

写真提供：AFP-jiji

野菜と果物と健康の秘密

56
023

Warm-up 1

音声を聴いて、写真を説明している英文を a ～ d から選びましょう。

a. ☐

b. ☐

c. ☐

d. ☐

57
024

Warm-up 2

メッセージを伝える「内容語」と呼ばれる名詞、動詞、形容詞、副詞には、通常強勢が置かれて発音されます。これが英語の独特のリズムを形成します。ここでは、動詞のいくつかを聴き取ってみましょう。日本語を参考に、（　　）内に当てはまる動詞を書き入れ、その後、音声を聴いて答えを確認し、リズムに注意して全文を読んでみましょう。

1. Consuming vegetables and fruits was confirmed to (　　　　　　　)
（　　　　　　　） the risk of early death among Japanese who eat a certain amount of them on a daily basis.

野菜や果物を摂取することが、日常的にそれらをある一定量食べている日本人の早期死亡のリスクを低減するのに役立っていることが確証された。

2. People who eat more fruits are 8 to 9 percent less likely to (　　　　　　　)
early than those who (　　　　　　　) little crops.

果物をたくさん食べる人は、それらの農産物（果物）をほとんど食べない人よりも早く死亡する可能性が 8 ～ 9% 低減される。

3. In the experiments, the amount and frequency of their consumption of vegetables and fruits were (　　　　　　　), so that respondents could be
（　　　　　　　） into five groups based on intakes of the crops.

実験では、野菜と果物の摂取量と摂取頻度が推定され、それらの農産物の摂取量に基づいて回答者らは 5 つのグループに分けられることになった。

Warm-up 3A

音声を聴いて、野菜と果物の摂取が人間の早期の死亡リスクを下げることがわかっ
たある調査の結果、最も死亡リスクを下げるための摂取量について述べられている
ものはどれか、1〜4から選びましょう。

1. 野菜と果物をそれぞれ300グラム食べる
2. 野菜を300グラムと果物を40グラム食べる
3. 野菜を300グラムまたは果物を114グラム食べる
4. 野菜を300グラムまたは果物を140グラム食べる

Warm-up 3B

以下の英文（果物と野菜の摂取と人の早期死亡リスクの関係について）を読み、質
問に答えましょう。

As veggies and fruits are rich in vitamins, minerals, dietary fiber and other nutrients, they are said to be good for the health.

Previous research on individuals in Europe and the United States had already found that consuming vegetables and fruits lessen the risk of early death. But the impact of eating the crops on Asian probability of early death had remained unclear, because their genetic backgrounds and lifestyles are different.

(The Asahi Shimbun)

Notes nutrient「栄養素」 lessen...「〜を低下させる」

Which of the following is NOT true about the relationship between people and the crops?

a. Consuming vegetables and fruits is considered to be healthy.
b. People in Europe and the United States eat more veggies and fruits than people in Asia.
c. The effects of eating such crops on Asian likelihood of early death had been unclear.
d. Previous research covered only individuals in Europe and the United States.

Study: Eating more veggies, fruit lowers early death risk of Japanese

In the first survey of its kind, consuming veggies and fruits was confirmed to help lower the risk of early death among Japanese who partook of them on a daily basis.

partake of... 「〜を食べる」

A team of researchers from the National Cancer Center and
5 Yokohama City University released its findings to support the crops' significance, while their potential health effects have traditionally been emphasized.

significance 「重要性」

"It is the first time that clear effects of vegetable and fruit consumption on the mortality risk have been reported in a study
10 targeting Japanese," said Atsushi Goto, an epidemiology professor at the university's Graduate School of Data Science, who was involved in the research.

mortality risk 「死亡リスク」
epidemiology 「疫学」

Tracking more than 90,000 individuals in Japan for 20 years, the correlations between the intake of vegetables and fruits and the
15 likelihood of early death were made clear through one of the nation's largest surveys.

correlation 「相関関係」
intake 「摂取量」
likelihood 「可能性」

The team conducted a questionnaire survey on the dietary habits of about 95,000 men and women between the ages 40 to 69 in 11 urban and rural locations nationwide in 1995 and 1998.

questionnaire 「アンケート」

20 The amount and frequency of their consumption of vegetables and fruits were estimated, so that respondents could be divided into five groups based on intakes of vegetables and also into five groups based on intakes of fruits. Their mortality risk was then assessed. About 24,000 individuals died during the 20-year research period.

assess... 「〜を評価する」

25 According to the outcomes, those who eat more fruits are 8 to 9 percent less likely to die early than those who consume little crops. A 7- to 8-percent risk improvement was seen among people who partake of more vegetables as well.

outcome 「結果」

By cause of death, having more fruits proved helpful in reducing
30 the likelihood of death associated with heart failure, myocardial infarction and other cardiovascular problems by 9 percent.

myocardial infarction 「心筋梗塞」
cardiovascular 「心臓血管に関わる」

(*The Asahi Shimbun* 一部抜粋・改変)

Comprehension

Choose two statements that are true about the passage.

1. In a survey targeting Japanese, clear effects of vegetable and fruit consumption on the mortality risk were reported for the first time.
2. The researchers tracked more than 90,000 individuals in Japan for three years.
3. The research team asked the men and women about their eating habits.
4. The respondents were divided into 10 groups based on their ages.
5. According to the results, those who consume more fruits are 8 to 9 percent less likely to die early than those who consume vegetables.

Summary

以下は本文の要約文です。1～4の空所に当てはまる語句を、選択肢から選び、書き入れましょう。

A team of researchers from the National Cancer Center and Yokohama City University released its report to support the (1.   ) of vegetables and fruits. They surveyed around 90,000 individuals in Japan for 20 years and confirmed the correlations between the intake of vegetables and fruits and the (2.   ) of their early death. The team conducted a (3.   ) survey on the dietary habits of the people in 1995 and 1998. The (4.   ) revealed that those who eat more fruits and vegetables are less likely to die early than those who consume little crops.

results	significance	questionnaire	likelihood

IT 技術で文化財を守る

 61
025

Warm-up 1

音声を聴いて、画像（登録有形文化財「大阪ガスビル」の３Ｄコンピュータグラフィック）を説明している英文を a ～ d から選びましょう。

a. ☐

b. ☐

c. ☐

d. ☐

 62
026

Warm-up 2

アメリカ英語では、母音に挟まれた t が破裂しないで、/d/ あるいは /r/ に近い音に発音される Flap T という現象があります。ただし、アクセントが t 直後の母音にある場合は、t をしっかりと発音します。日本語を参考に、音声を聴いて（　　　）内に当てはまる Flap T を含んだ語を書き入れましょう。その後、Flap T の発音に注意をして全文を読んでみましょう。

1. The three-dimensional (　　　　　　　　) are being used for such purposes as maintenance and the restoration of buildings damaged by disasters.

   その３Ｄデータは、建物のメンテナンスや災害で損傷を受けた建物の復旧などのような目的に活用されている。

2. The images of the Osaka Gas Building in Osaka City, a government-registered tangible cultural (　　　　　　　　) that was completed in 1933, can be seen on YouTube.

   1933 年に竣工した大阪市にある国の登録有形文化財「大阪ガスビル」の画像は、ユーチューブで見ることができる。

3. The images present a highly accurate reproduction of such details as (　　　　　　　　) on the walls.

   画像は、壁の模様など細部までかなり正確に再現している。

Warm-up 3A

音声を聴いて、1〜3の空所内に画像化技術の名前を書き入れましょう。

(1.) や (2.) をなどの画像化技術の飛躍的な進歩に
より、数年前から (3.) 技術の利用が急速に広がり始めている。

Warm-up 3B

以下の英文（建物の測量技術について）を読み、質問に答えましょう。

It is now possible to record the structures of buildings using 3D surveying technologies. Laser beams are projected onto the buildings from specialized devices, and the distance is measured to create three-dimensional shapes. Hundreds of millions of coordinate points are collected, and the 3D data are converted into CG images.

In conventional surveying, at least two people manually take measurements while confirming them against printed records. 3D scanning greatly improves efficiency and accuracy, and has therefore been widely introduced at construction sites.

(The Japan News)

 Notes surveying technology「測量技術」　project...「〜を照射する」　hundreds of millions of...「何億という〜」
coordinate points「座標点」　convert...into 〜「…を〜に変換する」　conventional「従来の」
manually「手作業で」　construction site「建築現場」

Which of the following is true about 3D surveying technology?

a. Laser beams are used to measure the distance from a target building.

b. It is difficult to measure buildings that are far away from the surveying equipment.

c. Two people are needed to operate the specialized devices.

d. The survey results should be checked against the printed records.

65 3D Data helps preserve historic buildings

Historically and architecturally important buildings are increasingly being preserved with the help of 3D data, as advancements in surveying technologies have made it possible to record not only the structure of a building but its exterior.

5 The data are being used for such purposes as maintenance and the restoration of buildings damaged by disasters.

Three-dimensional computer graphics of the Osaka Gas Building in Osaka City, a government-registered tangible cultural property that was completed in 1933, can be seen on YouTube. The images
10 present a highly accurate reproduction of such details as patterns on the walls, internal stairways and the shapes of pillars.

People involved in creating the graphics said elements such as the size and angle of inclination of the walls and pillars are accurate to within a few millimeters.

15 A technology called 3D scanning was used to create the graphics. Three-dimensional scanning was originally developed for the maintenance and management of buildings with high cultural value. Because such structures are usually not open to the public, the 3D images of Osaka Gas Building were put online so that as many
20 people as possible could see the building's interior.

The 3D data was created for the Osaka Gas Building by Kumonos Corp., a surveying company based in Mino, Osaka Prefecture. The company has produced 3D data for about 20 years, covering more than 2,000 projects.

25 Initially, 3D data of buildings were mainly used as basic data related to construction work. Recently, however, finished buildings are increasingly being recorded or promoted.

"Real buildings deteriorate, but 3D data can be passed on through the generations for cultural properties and other structures," a
30 Kumonos project chief said.

(*The Japan News* 一部抜粋・改変)

preserve...「〜を保存する」

exterior「外観」

stairway「階段」
pillar「柱」

angle of inclination「傾斜角」

originally「もともと」

initially「当初は」

promote...「〜を宣伝する」

deteriorate「劣化する」

Comprehension

Choose two statements that are true about the passage.

1. Three-dimensional scanning technologies to measure the structures of historic buildings have not been completed.
2. Three-dimensional scanning technologies cannot be used to restore buildings damaged by disasters.
3. The data produced by 3D scanning is extremely precise.
4. Kumonos Corp. has created 3D data for about two decades.
5. Three-dimensional data becomes worse with the passage of time, like real buildings.

Summary

以下は本文の要約文です。1～4の空所に当てはまる語を、最初の一文字をヒントにして書き入れましょう。

There is a growing trend to record historic buildings and famous architectural structures as 3D (1. d). Their structures and exteriors can be recorded (2. a) thanks to the advancements in surveying technologies. In addition to maintenance and management, the data can be used to restore buildings damaged by (3. d). The buildings are reproduced exactly as they were, with errors of no (4. m) than a few millimeters, such as the angle of inclination of walls and pillars.

写真提供：株式会社クモノス

Chapter

14

SDGs

「無駄」 にこそ意味あり

66
027

Warm-up 1 音声を聴いて、写真（コンテンツクリエーターの藤原麻里菜さんが、彼女が考えたイヤホンのケーブルを絡ませるマシーンの拡大版を展示場で披露している）を説明している英文を a 〜 d から選びましょう。

a. ☐

b. ☐

c. ☐

d. ☐

67
028

Warm-up 2 th の発音には濁らない / θ / と濁る /ð/ の 2 種類あります。日本語にはないこの音は上下の歯で舌先を軽く挟んで発音する摩擦音です。音声を聴いて 1 〜 3 の空所に当てはまる語を書き入れ、発音に気をつけて全文を読んでみましょう。

1. Fujiwara just made (　　　　　　　　) she wanted to make.

藤原さんは作りたいものを作っただけだった。

2. When fans asked if she would pose for photos with (　　　　　　　　),
Fujiwara smiled and flashed a peace sign.

ファンが自分たちと一緒に写真に写るポーズを取ってくれないかと頼むと、藤原さんは微笑んでピースサインをした。

3. One gadget pops up a model of (　　　　　　　) loading circle, which appears
on (　　　　　　) computer screen when (　　　　　　　) internet
connection is poor, in front of (　　　　　　) computer camera.

あるガジェットは、インターネットの接続が悪いときにコンピュータ画面に表示されるローディングサークルの模型をコンピュータのカメラの前に飛び出させる。

音声を聴いて、藤原麻里菜さんの経歴について<u>述べられていないもの</u>はどれか、1 〜 4 から選びましょう。

1. 高校卒業後、吉本総合芸能学院に入学した。
2. ピン芸人として活動していた。
3. あまり熱心に芸人活動をしていなかった。
4. 売れない芸人だった。

以下の英文（藤原麻里菜さんの無駄に対する考え）を読み、質問に答えましょう。

"When you find a stone on the roadside, you can touch it to see if it can be used as an interior decoration or as a paperweight, or you can refresh your mind by throwing it into a river," she said. "If you want to find usefulness in useless things, you need to have a tolerant mind and make use of their natural worthiness."

Her favorite phrase is: "Much more am I pleading for the abolition of the word 'use,' and for the freeing of the human spirit," which was said by U.S. chemist Abraham Flexner.

(The Asahi Shimbun)

 Notes **tolerant**「寛容な」 **worthiness**「有用性」 **plead for...**「〜を求める」 **use**「有用」

Which of the following is true about Fujiwara's opinion about uselessness?

a. She thinks that even a stone on the roadside is necessary for decorating a garden.
b. She finds uselessness in useful things.
c. She thinks it necessary to become tolerant to find usefulness in useless things.
d. She explains about uselessness by using a phrase of a U.S. inventor.

Ex-comedian shoots to fame with her beloved 'useless' gadgets

When Marina Fujiwara started showing off the elaborate "useless" inventions she made for fun, she did not expect to become a breakout internet star and amass a loyal following.

"I just make things I want to make," said Fujiwara, 29, who calls
5 herself the president of Kabushiki Gaisha Muda (Useless Ltd.). "I really don't know why my works are highly regarded."

She extolled the virtues of uselessness in person at an exhibition called "Kabushiki Gaisha Muda Shibuya Shiten" (Useless Ltd.'s Shibuya branch exhibition) in a corner of Tokyo's Shibuya Center-gai
10 street from August to September.

Fujiwara stood there sporting a stoic look while surrounded by some of her creations, of which she now has more than 200. When fans asked if she would pose for photos with them, Fujiwara smiled and flashed a peace sign.

15 "It is fascinating to see her churning out useless things like these when everything is supposed to be efficient nowadays," said a visitor with a smile.

She was referring to Fujiwara's works on display, including the "loading circle machine to escape from Zoom," a simple tool that
20 allows a person bored with an online drinking party to fake a frozen video connection.

"I made it because people told me they found it difficult to slip out of online drinking parties," Fujiwara said.

When the switch is pushed, the gadget pops up a model of the
25 loading circle, which appears on the computer screen when the internet connection is poor, in front of the computer camera.

Visitors to the exhibition appeared irritated but intrigued by an enlarged version of Fujiwara's "earphone cable entangling machine," which looked like a giant cable reel.

30 "It's fun to imagine what it feels like when something becomes extra-large," she said.

(*The Asahi Shimbun* 一部抜粋・改変)

Notes

shoot「突然～になる」
fame「人気、有名」

show off...「～を披露する」
elaborate「手の込んだ」

amass...「～を集める」
loyal「熱心な」

extol...「～を絶賛する」
virtue「良さ」

sport...「～を装う」

fascinating「魅力的な」
churn out...「～をたくさん作る」
be supposed to ...「～であることになっている」

refer to...「～に言及する」

slip out of...「～を抜け出す」

irritated「イライラしている」
intrigue...「～を興味を引く」
entangle「絡まる」

Comprehension

Choose two statements that are true about the passage.

1. Fujiwara used to work for a comedian.
2. She never imagined to be famous for her inventions.
3. She was surrounded by some fans at her exhibition.
4. One of the visitors to her exhibition said that it was fascinating to see Fujiwara creating useless things.
5. There were some visitors that showed irritation after seeing all her inventions.

Summary

以下は本文の要約文です。1〜4の空所に当てはまる語句を、選択肢から選び、書き入れましょう。

Marina Fujiwara has become famous for her (1.   ) "useless" inventions. She did not expect that her creations would attract so much attention. She held an exhibition and showed her works like an interesting tool that people can use when (2.   ) with an online drinking party to fake a (3.   ) video connection. Her earphone cable entangling machine irritated her visitors but made them (4.   ).

interested	frozen	elaborate	bored

環境・テクノロジー

日本の災害対策技術世界へ

 71
029
 Warm-up 1

音声を聴いて、写真（国連気候変動枠組み条約第27回締約国会議（COP27）の開催される会場について）を説明している英文を a ～ d から選びましょう。

a. ☐

b. ☐

c. ☐

d. ☐

写真提供：AP

 72
030
Warm-up 2

/r/ と /l/ の区別は日本人が苦手な発音の1つですが、/r/ の発音は日本語の「ウ」の口形で、舌をどこにもつけずに発音するのに対し、/l/ の発音は舌を上の歯の裏につけて発音します。音声を聴いて1～3の空所に当てはまる語を書き入れ、発音に気をつけて音読してみましょう。

1. An early warning system will help monitor heavy (   ) in developing countries reeling from the effects of global warming.

早期警戒システムが、地球温暖化の影響にあえいでいる新興国の豪雨を監視するのに役立つかもしれない。

2. The government hopes to (   ) the world's efforts to combat climate change.

日本政府は気候変動と戦う世界的な取り組みを主導したいと考えている。

3. According to a (   ) by the U.N. Intergovernmental Panel on Climate Change (IPCC), the frequency of extreme climate events will (   ) increase as temperatures (   ).

国連の気候変動に関する政府間パネル（IPCC）の報告書によると、気温が上昇するにつれて、異常気象の頻度がおそらく増すだろう。

Warm-up 3A 音声を聴いて、締約国会議（COP）の国連気候変動枠組み条約 (the United Nations Framework Convention on Climate Change) について<u>述べられていないもの</u>はどれか、1 〜 4 から選びましょう。

1. 今回の締約国会議は 27 回目である。
2. 国連気候変動枠組み条約には 189 の国や地域が参加している。
3. この会議では気候変動に対する対応策が話し合われる。
4. 国際社会は脱炭素に向けた取り組みが求められる。

 Note decarbonization「脱炭素」

 Warm-up 3B 以下の英文（国連気候変動枠組み条約に関する議論の焦点となる問題について）を読み、質問に答えましょう。

Developing countries have been strongly calling for assistance to deal with climate-related damage. How developed countries will respond to their calls will be a focus of this year's conference. In March, U.N. Secretary General Antonio Guterres stressed the need for widespread use of an early warning system, saying one-third of the world's population, mainly in developing countries, is not covered by such a system.

(The Japan News, The Associated Press)

 Notes respond to...「〜に応える」　Secretary General「事務総長」

Which of the following is NOT true about the passage?

a. Developing countries have been asking for help to cope with damage from climate change.

b. How developed countries will support developing countries will be a major topic of discussions.

c. The United Nations is asking one-third of the member countries to introduce an early warning system.

d. The U.N. Secretary General emphasized that it is also necessary to use an early warning system in developing countries.

75 # Govt to provide rainfall-warning tech to developing countries

The government will unveil a plan to support the rollout of an early warning system to monitor heavy rainfall in developing countries reeling from the effects of global warming at the U.N. Climate Change Conference (COP27), which will kick off Sunday in
5 Sharm El-Sheikh, Egypt.

The government hopes to lead the world's efforts to combat climate change by providing disaster prevention technologies and know-how cultivated in disaster-prone Japan.

Torrential rains, heat waves and droughts have been occurring
10 frequently around the world in recent years. According to a report by the U.N. Intergovernmental Panel on Climate Change (IPCC), the frequency of extreme climate events will likely increase as temperatures rise.

The human and economic impact of climate change tends
15 to be particularly extensive in developing countries where social infrastructure is fragile.

The government is considering creating a disaster warning system by utilizing small radars operated by Weathernews Inc., a Chiba-based weather data company. The radar can predict localized
20 torrential rains based on the development of clouds.

The government will also work with Japanese insurance companies to provide weather derivatives to help developing countries build economies that are more resilient to disasters.

Weather derivatives are a kind of damage insurance that provides
25 partial compensation in the event of a decline in agricultural or commercial production due to bad weather.

"We want to contribute to the support being offered to developing countries in cooperation with Japanese companies that have excellent technology and know-how. This will also lead to the
30 overseas expansion of these companies," Environment Minister Akihiro Nishimura told The Yomiuri Shimbun ahead of COP27.

(*The Japan News, The Associated Press* 一部抜粋・改変)

Notes

unveil... 「〜を発表する」
rollout 「導入」

kick off 「開幕する」

disaster-prone 「災害の多い」
torrential rain 「豪雨」
drought 「干ばつ」

extensive 「甚大な」

fragile 「脆弱な」

localized 「局所的な」

insurance 「保険」

derivative 「デリバティブ、派生商品」
resilient to... 「〜に柔軟に対応できる」

partial 「一部の」
compensation 「補償」
decline 「減少」

expansion 「展開、拡大」

Comprehension

Choose two statements that are true about the passage.

1. The Japanese government helps the world combat climate change by providing disaster prevention technologies and disaster-related know-how.
2. The Japanese government will support developing countries to introduce an early warning system to monitor heavy rainfall.
3. The IPCC report said that extreme climate events will likely raise temperatures.
4. Small radars that the government will use are operated by a Chinese weather data company.
5. Japanese insurance companies will also help developed countries to produce weather derivatives.

Summary

以下は本文の要約文です。1～4の空所に当てはまる語句を、選択肢から選び、書き入れましょう。

At the U.N. Climate Change Conference (COP27) held in Sharm El-Sheikh, Egypt, the Japanese government will (1.　　　　　　　) a plan to support the rollout of an early warning system to (2.　　　　　　) heavy rainfall in developing countries. The system includes small radars operated by a Japanese weather data company. The radar can (3.　　　　　　) localized torrential rains based on the development of clouds. Japanese insurance companies will also provide weather derivatives to help developing countries (4.　　　　　　) disaster-resistant economies.

> predict　　monitor　　unveil　　build

編著者

村尾純子（むらお　じゅんこ）

大阪工業大学准教授

深山晶子（みやま　あきこ）

大阪工業大学名誉教授

ソーシャル・パースペクティブ
―メディア英語で現代社会を読み解く

2024 年 2 月 20 日　第 1 版発行

編 著 者──村尾純子
　　　　　　深山晶子

発 行 者──前田俊秀

発 行 所──株式会社 三修社
　　　　　　〒 150-0001 東京都渋谷区神宮前 2-2-22
　　　　　　TEL03-3405-4511　FAX03-3405-4522
　　　　　　振替 00190-9-72758
　　　　　　https://www.sanshusha.co.jp
　　　　　　編集担当　菊池 暁　伊吹和真

印 刷 所──日経印刷株式会社

©2024 Printed in Japan　ISBN978-4-384-33527-9 C1082

表紙デザイン ── 峯岸孝之（Comix Brand）
本文 DTP　　── 川原田良一
準拠 CD 録音── ELEC
準拠 CD 製作── 高速録音株式会社
準拠 CD 吹込── Dominic Allen, Jennifer Okano

教科書準拠 CD 発売

本書の準拠 CD をご希望の方は弊社までお問い合わせください。

Vocabulary Quiz

Chapter 1　Vocabulary Quiz

A. 1 ～ 7 の語の意味を説明しているものを a ～ g の中から選び、（　　）内にその記号を書き入れましょう。

1. nutritious　　（　　　）
2. diagnose　　（　　　）
3. deficiency　　（　　　）
4. trigger　　（　　　）
5. tackle　　（　　　）
6. malnutrition　（　　　）
7. hunger　　（　　　）

    a. feeling of discomfort by lack of food
    b. to cause something to function
    c. full of nutrients or nourishment
    d. to make an effort to deal with a difficult problem
    e. to identify what the cause of a problem is
    f. lack of proper nutrition
    g. a lack or shortage

B. 1 ～ 3 の（　　）内に当てはまる表現を a ～ c から選び、必要なら形を変えて書き入れましょう。

1. TFT have helped provide a total of 6.8 million school meals to African and Asian children (　　　　　　　).
2. Anyone can post photos any number of times (　　　　　　　) charge.
3. The number of people (　　　　　　　) hunger reached 828 million globally since the outbreak of the pandemic.

    a. affect by
    b. free of
    c. in need

学籍番号	名前	Score
		╱10

Chapter 2　　Vocabulary Quiz

A. 1 ～ 7 の語の意味を説明しているものを a ～ g の中から選び、（　　　）内にその記号を書き入れましょう。

1. elucidate 　　　　（　　　　）
2. boost 　　　　　　（　　　　）
3. germination 　　　（　　　　）
4. unstable 　　　　　（　　　　）
5. concentration 　　（　　　　）
6. secrete 　　　　　（　　　　）
7. solution 　　　　　（　　　　）

    a. likely to change suddenly
    b. a liquid into which a solid has been mixed and has dissolved
    c. to make something clear
    d. a lot of something in one place
    e. to increase or improve something
    f. the process of a seed starting to grow
    g. to produce and release a liquid

B. 1 ～ 3 の（　　　）内に当てはまる表現を a ～ c から選び、書き入れましょう。

The researchers found that as (1. 　　　　　　　　　) rice plants was increased, (2. 　　　　　　　　　) strigolactone secreted per individual plant decreased, maintaining (3. 　　　　　　　　　) the hormone in the hydroponic environment.

    a. the same overall level of
    b. the number of
    c. the amount of

学籍番号	名前	Score
		/10

Chapter 3   Vocabulary Quiz

A. 1〜7の語の意味を説明しているものをa〜gの中から選び、(　　) 内にその記号を書き入れましょう。

1. multiply   (   )
2. evolve   (   )
3. laundry   (   )
4. atmosphere   (   )
5. effectively   (   )
6. target   (   )
7. premises   (   )

    a. to develop gradually from a simple to a more complicated form

    b. the building and land near to it that a business owns or uses

    c. to try to persuade a particular group of people

    d. the mood or feeling that exists in a place

    e. in a way that produces a successful result

    f. a facility where clothes are washed

    g. to increase in number

B. 1〜3の (　　) 内に当てはまる表現をa〜cから選び、必要なら形を変えて書き入れましょう。

1. More dual-income households use coin laundries to shorten the time spent on (   ).
2. On weekends, the coin laundry (   ) families.
3. Customers can wash sheets and futon covers (   ).

    a. bustle with

    b. all at once

    c. household chores

学籍番号	名前	Score
		/10

Chapter 4　　Vocabulary Quiz

A. 1〜7 の語の意味を説明しているものを a 〜 g の中から選び、(　　) 内にその記号を書き入れましょう。

1. trap　　　　(　　　)
2. potential　(　　　)
3. abdomen　(　　　)
4. hazardous　(　　　)
5. equipment　(　　　)
6. traverse　　(　　　)
7. remove　　(　　　)

    a. to prevent someone from leaving a place
    b. to move over something
    c. possible or likely in the future
    d. to take something away from a place
    e. dangerous especially to people's safety
    f. the things that are needed for a particular activity
    g. the end of an insect's body

B. 1〜3 の (　　) 内に当てはまる表現を a 〜 c から選び、必要なら形を変えて書き入れましょう。

1. The batteries inside small robots (　　　　　　　　) quickly.
2. When it (　　　　　　　) a cockroach's movements, the roach is causing itself to move.
3. The cockroaches can right themselves when (　　　　　　　).

    a. run out
    b. flip over
    c. come to

学籍番号	名前	Score
		10

Chapter 5 Vocabulary Quiz

A. 1～7の語の意味を説明しているものをa～gの中から選び、（　　）内にその記号を書き入れましょう。

1. correspondence （　　　　）
2. longhand （　　　　）
3. vanish （　　　　）
4. reveal （　　　　）
5. fictitious （　　　　）
6. recipient （　　　　）
7. figure （　　　　）

    a. not real
    b. to stop existing completely
    c. a person, especially a well-known one
    d. someone who receives something
    e. to let something become known
    f. ordinary writing by hand
    g. communication by letter or another form of written message

B. 1～3の（　　）内に当てはまる表現をa～cから選び、必要なら形を変えて書き入れましょう。

1. Previously, the correspondence sections of magazines used to be
（　　　　　　　　　　） the addresses of those looking for pen pals.
2. People who prefer to correspond without revealing their personal
information are （　　　　　　　） intermediate services.
3. Users can come in （　　　　　　　） the warmth of people through the
service.

    a. contact with
    b. fill with
    c. turn to

学籍番号	名前	Score
		╱10

Chapter 6   Vocabulary Quiz

A. 1 ～ 7 の語の意味を説明しているものを a ～ g の中から選び、（　　）内にその記号を書き入れましょう。

1. pharmacist　　（　　　）
2. prescription　　（　　　）
3. immune system　（　　　）
4. chat　　（　　　）
5. launch　　（　　　）
6. delivery　　（　　　）
7. payment　　（　　　）

   a. the act of taking goods, letters, etc. to people's houses
   b. a person who is trained to prepare and give out medicines in a hospital or shop
   c. to start
   d. the act of paying
   e. prescribed drug
   f. the body's cells and organs that fight illness and disease
   g. a friendly, informal conversation

B. ある女性患者について述べた、1 ～ 3 の英文の（　　）内に当てはまる表現を a ～ c から選び、必要なら形を変えて書き入れましょう。

1. A woman who (　　　　　　　) rheumatism has been using the service since the spring.
2. She visits a hospital two hours away and used to (　　　　　　　) her prescription at a pharmacy near there.
3. She also wanted to avoid (　　　　　　　) for long periods due to her compromised immune system.

   a. be outside
   b. suffer from
   c. pick up

学籍番号	名前	Score
		/10

Chapter 7   Vocabulary Quiz

A. 1 ～ 7 の語の意味を説明しているものを a ～ g の中から選び、（   ）内にその記号を書き入れましょう。

1. consume   (   )
2. nutrient   (   )
3. beverage   (   )
4. option   (   )
5. intake   (   )
6. ingredient   (   )
7. serving   (   )

    a. a substance that is needed to keep a living thing alive
    b. any type of drink except water
    c. something that you can choose in a particular situation
    d. one of the foods that you use in making a particular meal
    e. to eat or drink something
    f. an amount of food for one person
    g. the amount of something that you eat or drink

B. 1 ～ 3 の（   ）内に当てはまる表現を a ～ c から選び、必要なら形を変えて書き入れましょう。

1. She eats complete nutritional foods three to four times
    (   ) for breakfast.
2. The complete nutritional foods have (   ) flavors and types.
3. The product (   ) keep up with healthy eating.

    a. make it easy to
    b. a wide variety of
    c. a week

学籍番号	名前	Score
		/10

Chapter 8　Vocabulary Quiz

A. 1〜7 の語の意味を説明しているものを a 〜 g の中から選び、(　　) 内にその記号を書き入れましょう。

1. enthusiast　　　(　　　　)
2. benefit　　　　(　　　　)
3. eliminate　　　(　　　　)
4. process　　　　(　　　　)
5. excess　　　　(　　　　)
6. acquaintance　(　　　　)
7. contribute　　(　　　　)

    a.　to treat a substance with machines in order to make something
    b.　to give your time and effort in order to achieve something
    c.　someone who is very interested in something
    d.　much more than is necessary
    e.　to get rid of something that is not needed
    f.　to be helpful or useful
    g.　someone you know a little

B. 1〜3 の (　　) 内に当てはまる表現を a 〜 c から選び、必要なら形を変えて書き入れましょう。

1. Housebuilders nationwide have (1.　　　　　　　　　) Zanzai Bank to reuse scrap lumber.
2. Zanzai Bank projects are (2.　　　　　　　　) among small and midsize firms throughout the country.
3. According to the president of the company, about 6m³ of scrap wood is (3.　　　　　　　　) one house.

    a.　become widespread
    b.　start up
    c.　produce from

学籍番号	名前	Score
		/10

Chapter 9   Vocabulary Quiz

A. 1〜7の語の意味を説明しているものをa〜gの中から選び、（　　）内にその記号を書き入れましょう。

1. unscrew　　　（　　　）
2. invent　　　　（　　　）
3. face　　　　　（　　　）
4. inconvenience　（　　　）
5. exhibit　　　　（　　　）
6. motivation　　（　　　）
7. commercialize　（　　　）

    a. to start to deal with the situation

    b. to make something new

    c. to make a product available for sale to the public

    d. a reason or purpose for doing something

    e. to show or display in an exhibition or event

    f. a state or an example of problems or trouble, often causing a delay or loss of comfort

    g. to turn something until it comes out or off

B. 1〜3の（　　）内に当てはまる表現をa〜cから選び、必要なら形を変えて書き入れましょう。

1. The tool is (　　　　　　　　) by cutting a rubber tube into a 4-centimeter length.

2. She sold 280 of them in five days, (　　　　　　　　) all the materials she had prepared.

3. All you (　　　　　　　　) invent something is motivation and the ability to take action as soon as you hit upon an idea.

    a. use up

    b. make by hand

    c. need to

学籍番号	名前	Score
		/10

Chapter 10　Vocabulary Quiz

A. 1 ～ 7 の語の意味を説明しているものを a ～ g の中から選び、（　　）内にその記号を書き入れましょう。

1. exploration　　（　　　　）
2. infrastructure　（　　　　）
3. facilitate　　　（　　　　）
4. diameter　　　（　　　　）
5. essential　　　（　　　　）
6. quantify　　　（　　　　）
7. distribution　　（　　　　）

   a.　to make something possible or easier to happen
   b.　to express or measure the quantity of something
   c.　a trip to a place to discover something
   d.　the position or frequency of occurrence over an area
   e.　a straight line crossing a circle through the center
   f.　completely necessary
   g.　the basic facilities for the functioning of an area

B. 1 ～ 3 の（　　）内に当てはまる表現を a ～ c から選び、必要なら形を変えて書き入れましょう。

1. Attempts to set up lunar facilities (　　　　　　　　).
2. It takes approximately 27 days for the moon to rotate once
   (　　　　　　　　).
3. The facilities comprise a large glass-shaped structure measuring 200 to
   400 meters (　　　　　　　　).

   a.　on one's axis
   b.　be in full swing
   c.　in height

学籍番号	名前	Score
		⁄10

Chapter 11　Vocabulary Quiz

A. 1 ～ 7 の語の意味を説明しているものを a ～ g の中から選び、（　　）内にその記号を書き入れましょう。

1. delegate　　（　　　　）
2. lucrative　　（　　　　）
3. extinction　　（　　　　）
4. implement　　（　　　　）
5. depiction　　（　　　　）
6. predator　　（　　　　）
7. regulate　　（　　　　）

a. to control something
b. an animal that hunts, kills, and eats other animals
c. profitable
d. the way that something is represented or shown
e. a person sent to represent others
f. to start using a plan or system
g. a situation in which something no longer exists

B. 1 ～ 3 の（　　）内に当てはまる表現を a ～ c から選び、必要なら形を変えて書き入れましょう。

1. This historic decision will be remembered as the day we turned the tide to (　　　　　　　　) of the world's sharks and rays.
2. The proposal regarding the hammerhead shark (　　　　　　　　).
3. Sharks have (　　　　　　　　) in recent years.

a. undergo an image makeover
b. prevent the extinction
c. pass without debate

学籍番号	名前	Score
		/10

Chapter 12　　Vocabulary Quiz

A. 1〜7の語の意味を説明しているものをa〜gの中から選び、(　　) 内にその記号を書き入れましょう。

1. lessen　　　(　　　　)
2. correlation　(　　　　)
3. intake　　　(　　　　)
4. significance　(　　　　)
5. likelihood　(　　　　)
6. assess　　　(　　　　)
7. outcome　　(　　　　)

    a. importance
    b. the chance that something will happen
    c. a connection or relationship between two or more facts, numbers, etc.
    d. a result or effect of an action
    e. to make something smaller
    f. to judge or decide the amount, value, quality, or importance of something
    g. the amount of a particular substance that is eaten or drunk

B. 1〜3の(　　) 内に当てはまる表現をa〜cから選び、必要なら形を変えて書き入れましょう。

1. Consuming veggies and fruits was confirmed to help lower the risk of early death among Japanese who (　　　　　　　) them on a daily basis.
2. The relationship between the consumption of crops and the death risk was (　　　　　　　) through a survey.
3. Eating more fruits proved helpful in reducing the likelihood of death (　　　　　　　) heart failure by 9 percent.

    a. associate with
    b. partake of
    c. make clear

学籍番号	名前	Score
		/10

Chapter 13　　Vocabulary Quiz

A. 1 ～ 7 の語の意味を説明しているものを a ～ g の中から選び、（　　）内にその記号を書き入れましょう。

1. preserve　　　　（　　　　）
2. structure　　　　（　　　　）
3. restoration　　　（　　　　）
4. detail　　　　　（　　　　）
5. initially　　　　（　　　　）
6. construction　　（　　　　）
7. deteriorate　　　（　　　　）

    a. something large such as a building that is built from different parts
    b. to become worse
    c. to take care of something to prevent it from being destroyed
    d. the work of building something
    e. at the beginning
    f. one of many small pieces of information
    g. the act of putting something back into its original condition

B. 1 ～ 3 の（　　）内に当てはまる表現を a ～ c から選び、必要なら形を変えて書き入れましょう。

1. According to the people (　　　　　　　　) creating the graphics, the elements of the building are accurate to within a few millimeters.
2. The building is not (　　　　　　　) the public.
3. The 3D data of the building was (　　　　　　　) basic data related to construction work.

    a. involve in
    b. use as
    c. open to

学籍番号	名前	Score
		╱10

Chapter 14　Vocabulary Quiz

A. 1〜7の語の意味を説明しているものを a〜g の中から選び、（　　）内にその記号を書き入れましょう。

1. tolerant　　（　　　）
2. worthiness　（　　　）
3. fame　　　　（　　　）
4. elaborate　　（　　　）
5. amass　　　　（　　　）
6. churn out　　（　　　）
7. intrigue　　　（　　　）

    a. how suitable someone or something is
    b. able to continue existing despite bad or difficult conditions
    c. to produce large amounts of something quickly
    d. the state of being known or recognized by many people
    e. containing a lot of careful detail or many detailed parts
    f. to interest someone a lot
    g. to get a large amount of something

B. 1〜3の（　　）内に当てはまる表現を a〜c から選び、必要なら形を変えて書き入れましょう。

1. Marina Fujiwara started (　　　　　　　　　) the useless inventions that she made for fun on the internet.
2. Everything (　　　　　　　) be efficient nowadays.
3. People found it difficult to (　　　　　　　) online drinking parties.

    a. slip out of
    b. show off
    c. be supposed to

学籍番号	名前	Score
		／10

Chapter 15 Vocabulary Quiz

A. 1〜7の語の意味を説明しているものをa〜gの中から選び、（　　）内にその記号を書き入れましょう。

1. widespread （　　　）
2. rollout （　　　）
3. reveal （　　　）
4. drought （　　　）
5. kick off （　　　）
6. fragile （　　　）
7. resilient （　　　）

    a. to make known to others
    b. the act of making something, especially a product or service, available for the first time
    c. to begin or start
    d. a long period of abnormally low rainfall
    e. able to recover quickly from difficult conditions
    f. distributed over a large area or number of people
    g. easily broken

B. 1〜3の（　　）内に当てはまる表現をa〜cから選び、必要なら形を変えて書き入れましょう。

1. The human and economic impact of climate change (　　　　　　　　) be particularly extensive in developing countries.
2. The radar can predict localized torrential rains (　　　　　　　) the development of clouds.
3. The government will also (　　　　　　　) Japanese insurance companies to provide weather derivatives to developing countries.

    a. base on
    b. tend to
    c. work with

学籍番号	名前	Score
		╱10